The Four Skills of Cultural Diversity Competence

A Process for Understanding and Practice

The Four Skills of Cultural Diversity

A Process for Understanding and Practice

Mikel Hogan-Garcia
California State University, Fullerton

Brooks/Cole • Wadsworth

I(T)P® An International Thomson Publishing Company

Belmont • Albany • Bonn • Boston • Cincinnati • Detroit • Johannesburg • London • Madrid • Melbourne
Mexico City • New York • Pacific Grove • Paris • Singapore • Tokyo • Toronto • Washington

Sponsoring Editor: *Eileen Murphy*
Editorial Assistant: *Julie Martinez*
Production Editor: *Tessa McGlasson Avila*
Manuscript Editor: *Lorraine Anderson*
Permissions Editor: *Connie Dowsett*
Interior Design: *Ellen Pettengell*

Cover Design: *Jamie Dagdigian*
Cover Illustration: *Kerry Townsend Smith*
Indexer: *James Minkin*
Typesetting: *Thompson Type*
Printing and Binding: *Webcom, Limited*

For more information, contact:

WADSWORTH PUBLISHING COMPANY
10 Davis Drive
Belmont, CA 94002
USA

International Thomson Publishing
Europe
Berkshire House 168-173
High Holborn
London WC1V 7AA
England

Thomas Nelson Australia
102 Dodds Street
South Melbourne 3205
Victoria, Australia

Nelson Canada
1120 Birchmount Road
Scarborough, Ontario
Canada M1K 5G4

International Thomson Editores
Seneca, 53
Colonia Polanco
11560 México, D.F., México
C.P. 11560

International Thomson Publishing GmbH
Königswinterer Strasse 418
53227 Bonn
Germany

International Thomson Publishing Asia
60 Albert Street
#15-01 Albert Complex
Singapore 189969

International Thomson Publishing Japan
Hirakawacho Kyowa Building, 3F
2-2-1 Hirakawacho
Chiyoda-ku, Tokyo 102
Japan

Printed in Canada

10   9   8   7   6   5   4   3

Library of Congress Cataloging-in-Publication Data

Hogan-Garcia, Mikel, [date]
    The four skills of cultural diversity competence: a process for
understanding and practice / Mikel Hogan-Garcia.
        p.   cm.
    Includes bibliographical references and index.
    ISBN 0-534-34301-5
    1. Multiculturalism.   2. Ethnicity.   3. Culture conflict.
4. Communication and culture.   5. Interpersonal communication.
I. Title.
HM276.H734   1998
306—dc21
                                                        98-34854
                                                            CIP

This book is dedicated to my brother, Matt Hogan, Ph.D.,
University of Wisconsin, Madison

Contents

List of Tables
and Worksheets

Preface

The Four Skills of Cultural Diversity Competence introduces a process that opens the reader to growth in intercultural skills. It conducts the user through an educational training program specifically designed to initiate ongoing preparation for effective interaction with culturally diverse people. Growth in these skills equips individuals with the social and emotional grace they need in order to form the bonds of mutual trust and confidence that will bridge the differences that ordinarily divide people.

My life experience, growing up and living in Southern California, made it clear to me that intercultural skills grow only through information and practice—that they seldom occur naturally in culturally diverse societies. I use some of my own childhood experiences to illustrate the theoretical premises of the educational and training process set forth in this book.

Although much of the United States can be described as culturally diverse, post-war Southern California is remarkable for the intensity and depth of its cultural diversity. It was in this rich multicultural setting, during the 1950s and 1960s, that the seeds of my awareness for the need for cultural skills were first sown.

Surprisingly, my learning began as a result of the absence of intercultural knowledge and skill, rather than because of its practice. At that time, culturally diverse people lived in their own socially demarcated worlds, so intercultural communication was simply not happening. We did not enter into the process of shared information and effective interaction because we did not involve ourselves in intercultural relationships, where intercultural communication could take place. And to compound this situation further, we didn't even realize there was a problem. Woven into the very fabric of normal everyday life was the reality that Black people lived in their part of the town, Asian people in theirs, Latinos in theirs, and White western European-American people, in theirs. If anyone called attention to this state of affairs, our typical response would have been, "Where's the problem?" This is a classic example of cognitive blind-sight, and its resultant denial.

The following story will help to illustrate my point further. I grew up in a middle-class suburb, by and large western European-American in its collective ethnicity. Within my community I regularly received quite contradictory cultural messages from my seemingly humanistic and liberal elders. For example, I heard such things as, "Don't worry about the clothes people wear or the color of their skin," all that matters is "if you like them" as people. Yet when my brother and I suggested we bring home a Black friend, we witnessed our parents recoiling in shock and fear. "We cannot bring Negroes here into our home; the neighbors won't like it. We have to live in this neighborhood." I had thought that Black/White racism stopped in the South and "fairness" reigned outside that region. I was confused at the mixed messages. It was not until later, when I was in college, that I reflected on that incident and realized that racism and cultural intolerance was present in my own home.

Sadly, such contradictions were the norm for me, and I saw this more clearly as the years passed. The words and behaviors I witnessed as a girl ranged from simple intolerance of difference to outright bigotry. My maternal grandmother told me that "nigras" don't have souls, so they can't go to heaven. There were the critical scowls and cutting disapproval of my Protestant grammar-school friends when confronted with my Irish Catholic practices. And then, in turn, the cruel grilling those same friends would receive from my Irish Catholic grandmother, when she was introduced to them and their names were anything but Irish: "Hmmm, my now, what's that name," she would unashamedly ask them, "English? German? Why, there's no Irish in that name!" I remember the rude stares at the birthmark on my side whenever I wore a two-piece bathing suit to the beach, and the startled responses and direct denials that even my name could generate. No one except my immediate family could believe that my name was really "Mikel." "Why, that's a boy's name," they'd say. Once my mother had to admonish the nuns at St. Anthony's when they insisted on calling me "Michele."

My parents were, however naively, committed to education and cultural refinement, for themselves and their five children. When I was thirteen they treated some of us to a fascinating and joy-filled six-week car tour of the length and breadth of Mexico. It was a fabulous trip, and one that I will never forget. But imagine my confusion, after being exposed to the rich cultures of Mexico, to return to school only to hear the derisive comments about Mexicans; this, in a Catholic school with a substantial Latino population. Then, later, my family's grimaces and discomfort, and even denial, that my boyfriend (eventual husband) was Mexican-American, and the frequent discrimination we experienced in public when we went out as Mr. and Mrs. Garcia in the Los Angeles metropolitan area of the mid-1960s.

When I was growing up, I was taught that regardless of race, color, ethnicity, creed, or other orientation, all that was really required for anyone to get on well in this land was hard work and an education, so for years I presumed a level playing field for all in the United States. Such notions of the existence of a great meritocracy formed the interpretive framework of my thinking, whatever the myriad contradictions I encountered in my daily life. And then there was Watts in 1965! The violence of this rebellion, for that is what it was, served to shatter any illusions I may have harbored about the myth of the great American meritocracy. No longer could I be told to "hush," or be put off with "well, that's different," because my experiences simply failed to match the myth.

By the late 1960s, in college, I found a fertile and tolerant ground to more freely explore the great puzzlement I felt about people and culture in general. Anthropology with its rich resource of cultural theories and concepts quite understandably captured and held my interest, and won my devotion. The more I worked the more I realized that this field offered the best approach for me to expand my understanding of culture and the human question. In college I became increasingly aware that, throughout my life, I had been marginalized, and it was through the utilization of the anthropological method of inquiry that I found a constructive way to explore that sense of marginality.

Anthropology, as a discipline, supplied the theoretical foundation for my work of exploration, but my investigation of diverse meanings did not stop there. Beyond academic study and theory, my investigatory work took a very active professional turn. Early on, my interests, quite naturally, led me into work with the Fair Housing Foundation of Long Beach. Later, I acted as Program Coordinator for Project Equity, a desegregation center located on the Cal State University, Fullerton, campus that offered assistance to schools K-12. And it was through these affiliations that I began working with the Coalition for Children, Adolescents, and Parents (CCAP) in the culturally diverse communities of Orange County. CCAP aims to prevent teen pregnancy and other "at risk" behaviors. Simultaneously, I founded the certificate program at Cal State University, Fullerton, entitled "Managing for Excellence with Culturally Diverse Employees and Customers" while continuing to teach university classes in anthropology and human services, always with an emphasis on race, ethnic, and gender relations.

Goal of the Book

So, it is in this developmental context that my own sense of cultural awareness and understanding struck root and grew to include direct and specific problem solving in real communities, as well as strategic planning in actual community development projects. These are the goals that encompass something more than mere cultural awareness and understanding. My goals focus on cultural awareness and understanding that actually lead to the establishment of culturally effective techniques and processes that will routinely succeed in real communities. I have always aimed for cultural techniques and processes that succeed in real communities, that allow people to maintain pride in themselves and their cultures of origin, as well as any other groups or associations with which they regularly identify as they interact with others.

The specific techniques and processes I envision enable those who participate to appreciate another person's freedom to think and act differently. In other words, participants can agree to disagree. My techniques and processes enable participants to see that it is okay to differ, that difference is, in fact, something to be enjoyed, and that it is from difference itself that significant learning about oneself and one another eventually arises. These are the ground rules for productive interaction and exchange that effectively dissolve the sources of confusion, numbness, conflict, and festering animosity.

The Four Skills of Cultural Competence provides the reader with a step-by-step format for entering into and developing cultural competence. The process my book sets forth results from and draws strongly on my cultural diversity work over the past twenty years. It is based on a fundamental premise: Cultural competence is an ongoing and multilayered process that involves personal, interpersonal, and organization-wide levels—and is always in the moment.

The book describes an education and training process for developing cultural competence: the ability to interact effectively with culturally diverse people. Culturally diverse people are those whose acquired knowledge is different and who thus behave and interpret experience differently. Because our communities are becoming ever more culturally diverse, cultural competence is a necessity.

Who the Book Is Intended For

Since the book provides an adaptable four-skills approach to diversity competence development, it can be used by educators teaching in K-12 schools. Learning pro-active ways of thinking about and communicating with diverse others is useful for preventing, defusing, and reducing conflicts at schools. Since there is a trend in colleges and universities to link academic education with job skills, this book is highly recommended to all courses in the Social Services and Humanities. For example, this book can be used as I do in Human Services and Anthropology courses for promoting the integration of theory and practice into a much needed and highly marketable job skill.

Professional trainers and Human Resources personnel will also find the book useful in a range of work organizations: corporate training in business, nonprofit community agencies, and government offices, as well as medical facilities.

My Approach to the Subject

Being an anthropologist, I study human culture in its myriad forms: different ways of thinking and perceiving, different customs, and different communication systems and styles. Our communities are composed of people from diverse cultures who are thrust together in jobs, schools, and neighborhoods without effective ways of thinking or speaking across the diversity. To a great extent, people today are begin placed into anthropological fieldwork situations without the personal interest, training, understanding, or communication skills.

I approach cultural diversity competence as multilevel. My approach encompasses cultural awareness, understanding, and skills at the personal, interpersonal, and organization-wide levels. The first two skills increase cultural awareness and understanding, and the third and fourth skills foster effective interpersonal skills and organization-change strategies. Each chapter combines both cognitive and experiential learning. Following adult learning principles, I assume cultural competence is acquired through a practice or dual exercise of action and reflection. With coaching, feedback, and self-reflection, in other words, one learns to be and to behave in a culturally competent manner.

Organization, Scope, and Content of the Text

In the Introduction I describe the context and need for cultural diversity competence, based on the very real change observable in our jobs and communities. In line with this context and need, I then offer an overview of the four skills development process. Chapter Two introduces and demonstrates Skill One: Understanding Culture as It Operates on Different Social Levels. Chapter Three does the same with Skill Two: Understanding Common Barriers to Effective Communication and Relationships. Together, Skill One and Skill Two form the "cultural mindedness" that is the foundation for effective interactions, the subject of Chapter Four. In Chapter Four, Skill Three is introduced and demonstrated: Practicing Personal and Interpersonal Cultural Performance. We move on to Skill Four in Chapter Five: Practicing the Design and Implementation of Organizational Strategies and Action Plans. Each chapter provides worksheets and discussion sheets designed to demonstrate the information presented on the four skills.

Learning Aids, Pedagogical Structures, and Other Features

In each chapter, worksheets accompany presentation of each skill. The instructor's manual includes pedagogical explanations, suggested activities, overhead transparencies, study questions, and chapter outlines and key terms, and is also available electronically, in ASCII format.

The following reviewers lent their expertise to the project, and I thank them: Patricia Hudson, The George Washington University; Donna Henderson, Wake Forest University; Theresa Bowman Downing, Thomas Edison State College.

Mikel Hogan-Garcia

Chapter 1

Introduction

Context

In recent years, recognition of the need for cultural-diversity awareness and skill has grown in the workplace. This cultural awareness,
coupled with the skills needed to interact successfully with people of
diverse cultural backgrounds who work in the same place, is called
diversity competence or *cultural competence*. These terms imply the un-
derlying qualities of awareness, understanding, and skill (Bach, 1993;
Foster et al., 1988; Hudson Institute, 1987; Lamphere, 1992; Pederson,
1988, p. 115).

Often the cultural awareness and skills that make a person "diversity
competent" are simply lacking today. Where this is the case, a kind of
operational gridlock can occur, at great cost to the workplace. These
circumstances in the workplace have stimulated the concern and interest of people engaged in business, education, health, and human services, and has led to an increasing emphasis on the formal training of
employees in cultural competence.

This interest and emphasis centering on diversity competence training are clearly a response to a felt need. This need is itself a response to
a twofold national and global change: our communities and our work
domains are increasingly diverse, both socially and culturally, and the
rate of social and economic change is accelerating. Take, for example,
work-force composition: just a generation ago White males were, and
were thought of as, the mainstay of the economy. Today, alongside
White males, White females, immigrants, and a large mix of traditional
ethnic groups (Blacks, Latinos, Asians, Native Americans, and Pacific
Islanders) have taken their own place in the work force (Goldstein &
Leopold, 1990; Nelton, 1988; Thomas, 1996).

This accelerating rate of social, economic, and cultural change is a
distinct and important factor explaining the increased need for cultural-

competence training. Researchers Donald Schon (1971) and Ralph Kill-man (1987) described in the 1970s and 1980s how, as a nation, we no longer lived in a "steady state," but in an "era of dynamic complexity." It is thus a strategic imperative for our sociocultural system to adapt by instituting flexible synergistic (internally cooperative) organizations and institutions, as Killman makes clear:

> Creating and then maintaining organizational success is a different kind of problem from that of only a few decades ago. The world has grown increasingly complex—resulting from the greater interdependence among world economies. At the same time the world has become increasingly dynamic—resulting from the information explosion and worldwide communications. This "dynamic complexity" means that organizations cannot remain stable for very long. *Rather, constant change on the outside requires constant change on the inside.* Success is largely determined by how well the organization adjusts all its tangible and intangible properties to keep itself on track with its surroundings. (1987, pp. 2–3; *italics mine*)

Need

In order, then, to respond in an adaptive way to this sociocultural change, we have the task of transforming our organizations and institutions into more flexible systems. Such systems would be adaptive in the sense of being proactive (anticipatory and timely) rather than merely reactive. Our organizations and institutions, adaptive in this sense, need to be able continually to restructure themselves in response to a constantly changing, unpredictable environment (Hamada & Sibley, 1994; Jordan, 1994; Kanter, 1977, 1983, 1989; Killman, 1987; Morgan & Ramirez, 1983; Schon, 1987; Schwartzman, 1993; Wright, 1994).

Organizations and institutions, however, cannot respond in a proactive manner unless employees at every level develop new, culturally appropriate communication skills. The development of such skills allows for the emergence of collaborative, interdependent team relationships. The emergence of this kind of *synergistic* team relationship provides in turn for the emergence of truly synergistic organizations and institutions. The teamwork that characterizes such organizations and institutions makes them fully capable of continually producing strategies that respond dynamically to ever-changing environmental conditions.

In other words, for such synergistic organizations to develop, it is essential for everyone in the organizations to develop a new and different mode of interacting with one another. This new and different mode of interaction needs to be one that *values* diversity and that responds not just reactively but proactively to ongoing change—that is, that *anticipates* change. This mode of interacting fosters understanding among people, and understanding is a basic dynamic in the development of teamwork. This is so because teamwork—*synergy*—is only possible if people treat each other with respect and can communicate effectively one with another. This is precisely the challenge facing the workplace (as well as society and humankind as a whole): people need to design effective strategies for dealing with the phenomenon of ever-increasing cultural diversity in the midst of constant change (Eddy & Partridge, 1987; Kogod, 1994; Thomas, 1996; Wulff & Fiske, 1987).

This dynamic phenomenon of increasing diversity in the midst of constant change has challenged us for at least the last couple of decades, and it is not likely to disappear. Cultural diversity itself, if we can only acknowledge it, actually provides a rich resource of alternative ideas and ways of doing things, as well as significant points of contact with virtually all the nations of the world. It should be clear that this re-source, this *human* resource, provides a practical means of developing flexible and creative strategies for timely response to constant environmental change. In this sense, it provides us with a real basis for hope— certainly for better success in managing our business affairs, but also for managing our very survival on this planet. At this stage, business and survival are vitally linked (Bodley, 1996). However, to tap into and enliven this human resource, cultural competence is necessary. The present workbook offers a practical hands-on process for developing the four basic skills of cultural competence.

In line with this, Worksheet 1 will help you experience in a more direct fashion your own personal grounding as regards change in cultural diversity and the dynamic aspects of teamwork.

Worksheet 1

Context and Need (approx. total time 40 mins.)

Purpose To demonstrate current context of population diversity and fast pace of change, and to establish need for cultural competence.

Instructions Form groups of two to four persons. Discuss items 1 and 2 below and list pertinent examples for each item.

1. Have you witnessed any examples of change and/or cultural diversity in the last two years? Please list. (approx. 10 mins.)

   Example: The new computer system (Windows 95) the university is currently implementing throughout the faculty offices on campus. Or, on the level of cultural diversity, the increase in my classes of students from Russia, Romania, and Croatia. I have had approximately ten students, new immigrants from those countries, in the last three years.

   _____

   _____

   _____

   _____

   _____

2. Have you been in a situation in which you worked as a member of a team? If yes, please describe that experience briefly in the space below. (approx. 10 mins.)

   Example: I have served as coordinator for a committee in charge of writing a new interdisciplinary course of instruction for our school of Human Development and Community Service. Since the committee's members are from different disciplines, the completion of our task requires we work cohesively as a team.

   _____

   _____

   _____

   _____

   _____

Debriefing Questions

Write your answers to the debriefing questions individually in the spaces that follow. (approx. 20 mins.)

1. Did you have any personal reactions to items 1 and 2?

2. What did you learn about yourself from this activity?

3. What did you learn about others?

4. Name two ways you can use this learning in daily life.

An Overview of the Training Process

The problems facing our society, its institutions and organizations, are multileveled: they are personal, interpersonal, organizational, and institutional. This means that a training model designed to address these problems must itself be multileveled in these ways. The training model described here is designed as just such a multileveled training process. This training process, sometimes also referred to as holistic, guides individuals in the work of learning how to *recognize* and *value* diversity in other people. As this kind of recognition and respect grows, individuals learn to foster and expand their ability to interact effectively with people of diverse backgrounds and with diverse ways of doing things.

This dual process of learning to value and respect diversity and thereby growing in the ability to deal with it more effectively, provides the *interpersonal* basis or foundation for fundamentally changing our organizations and institutions into more collaborative, synergistic structures. The broad objective, therefore, of the present training model in cultural competence is to work on a person-to-person basis to refashion our hierarchical social structures into more collaborative, synergistic collectives. Such collectives base themselves on teamwork and have proven themselves much less wasteful of personnel than their hierarchically structured counterparts (Fernandez, 1991; Jamieson & O'Mara, 1991; Kanter, 1977, 1983, 1989; Loden & Rosener, 1991; Morgan & Ramirez, 1983; Morrison, 1992; Rosener, 1998; Thomas, 1996).

The process set in motion by this training model grounds itself in the three dynamic anthropological principles of self-reflection, emic contextualization, and implementation of change through a holistic or systems approach (Hogan-Garcia, 1991, 1995). Briefly stated, *self-reflection* is an active process of understanding oneself over one's life cycle. *Emic contextualization* is a process of obtaining information on attitudes, value orientations, and social relations from the inside, directly from the people involved in the situation at hand. A *holistic or systems approach* to change is a process in which there is serious systemwide planning, implementation, and evaluation of organization policies and procedures in relation to organization goals. This holistic approach also requires scrutiny of the organization from within the political and economic context of the wider sociocultural system of which the organization is a part. These three dynamic anthropological principles naturally correspond to the personal, interpersonal, and organizational levels—levels at which barriers typically exist that regularly block effective human relations and communication within hierarchically ordered organizations.

The training model, as represented in Table 1, consists of two broadly interdependent components—one's cultural knowledge or "cultural mindedness" (column 2), and one's action/skills (column 3), which

Table 1 *A Training Model for Cultural Diversity Competence*

Anthropological Principles	Cultural Knowledge	Action/Skills
Level 1: Personal level Self-reflection →	Personal culture (core identity) →	Personal competencies
↓	↓	↓
Level 2: Interpersonal level Emic contextualization →	Specific cultures • U.S. mainstream • Ethnic subcultures →	Skills to obtain accurate cultural information • Dialogue • Conflict recovery • Problem solving
↓	↓	↓
Level 3: Organizational level Holistic/systems approach	Organizational culture • Policies • Procedures • Programs • Processes	Organizational change Strategies and action plans

include verbal and nonverbal communication skills. These two broad components are multileveled in that they flow directly from the three anthropological principles just discussed (column 1). The two components of the process of change as represented in columns 2 and 3 (that is, one's cultural knowledge and one's action/skills) can be viewed, then, as an experiential application of the anthropological principles represented in column 1. Table 1, then, schematically represents the process of change insofar as it encompasses each individual's work at self-reflection for change, all individuals' interpersonal work at emic contextualization for change, and the organization's holistic systems approach to change.

The outcome of all this complex and combined effort is cultural diversity competence at the individual level, effective relationships at the interpersonal level, and culturally competent organizations at the systems level. The first broad component (cultural mindedness) increases cultural understanding, and the second (interpersonal relationship skills) engages participants in practicing interpersonal skills based on the expanded cultural understanding they have achieved.

Change at the Organizational Level: A Model

When working with organizations in the throes of change, I have regularly found it helpful to envision the organizational change process as taking place in four stages. Stage 1 is a stage of relative equilibrium. In stage 1, the organization functions in a relatively smooth manner until some factor such as a marked increase in employee diversity destabilizes the organization's functionality. As the intensity of conflict increases due to lack of understanding and miscommunication, the organization enters a second stage, sometimes referred to as the storming stage. The storming stage is marked by a high level of organization-wide conflict and is a critical stage; depending on, for example, the interpersonal processes employed at stage 2, the organization can remain mired in pervasive conflict with reaction becoming the norm, and death or a state of ongoing organization dysfunction the outcome. If there is leadership with vision, however, in which proactive processes—such as diversity competence training for employees—are widely implemented, members of the organization can learn to work together successfully through the crisis. The ability to work through problems in a proactive manner is itself the third stage, called the proactive problem-solving stage. In this way, over time, the organization can attain a new relative equilibrium, the fourth stage (Rosen, 1991; Smith, 1993).

Change at the Individual Level: A Model

Change at the individual level is also a process, a process of self-reflection concerning the actualization of the fourteen competencies or personal-level skills for change (see pp. 61–62). Actualization of these competencies involves a twofold dynamic within the person of recognition and subsequent personal behavior modification. All of this individual work becomes intrapersonal in the context of the human organization itself in the process of change. In trying to envision this self-reflective behavioral process on the individual level, I have found it helpful to think of it in terms of gradations in the intensity, duration, and frequency of the individual's recognitions and behavior modifications (Malott, Tillema, & Glenn, 1978).

The Interactive Learning Mode

The mode or instructional approach of this training process is interactive—that is, it combines both cognitive and experiential learning. Following adult learning principles, I assume cultural competence is acquired through a practice of action and reflection. In other words, with coaching, feedback, and self-reflection, one learns to be and to behave in a diversity-competent manner by doing diversity-competent things (Brookfield, 1990; Hogan-Garcia, 1991; Mehr, 1992; Sikkema & Niyekawa, 1987).

Table 2 *The Cultural Diversity Competence Change Process*

Stages	Skills
1	Self-reflection (personal awareness and understanding)
	↓
2	Personal competencies (personal behavioral skills)
	↓
3	Interpersonal diversity competence (interpersonal relationship skills)
	↓
4	Effective teamwork (interpersonal and group relationship skills)
	↓
5	Organizational cultural competence (skills in valuing and utilizing cultural diversity)

Cultural competence is an interpersonal skill, and, as in the case of all skills, acquiring it is a long-term process. It is best, for these reasons, to think of it as a lifelong practice, a lifelong learning exercise. The more we practice diversity competency skills, the sharper they become and the more reflexively, spontaneously, and automatically we behave in a cultural-competent manner.

Table 2 represents the stages in the change process toward becoming culturally competent individuals and organizations. The actual process, it must be remembered, is an *organic* process in which the stages unfold and interrelate dynamically in a forward-and-back, overlapping manner. Each of us, as we grow more and more culturally competent, provides the human infrastructure for developing culturally competent organizations, insofar as their policies, procedures, programs, and processes come to value and utilize cultural diversity.

In this introduction, we have described the context and need for cultural diversity competence as based in the very real change observed in organizations and the world around us. In line with this context and need, we have offered an overview of the training process we are proposing for implementing a proactive holistic program for responding to these assumed circumstances of change. We have also offered preliminary models for envisioning change on the organizational and individual levels. We concluded with a discussion of the interactive nature of the training process embodied in this book. In Chapter 2 we introduce and demonstrate skill 1: understanding culture as it operates on different social levels.

Chapter 2
Skill One

Understanding Culture as It Operates on Different Social Levels

The Concept of Culture

When thinking about the concept of culture, it is most important to avoid the traditional definition that assumes a stability, coherence, and homogeneity in the patterns of social groups and their behavior, because this kind of definition can result in troublesome and fruitless stereotyping (Hill-Burnett, 1987, pp. 123–140). Leininger (1995, p. 9) suggests a more useful definition of culture as "learned, shared, and transmitted values, beliefs, norms, and lifeways of a designated group which are generally transmitted intergenerationally and influence one's thinking and action modes."

Two broad properties of culture are especially relevant for developing cultural competence:

1. Culture is both subjective and objective.
2. Culture is multileveled and dynamic.

Culture as Subjective and Objective

Culture is both subjective and objective in that it is comprised of a meaning system (subjective) that dictates how and why to behave in a certain way, the objective component. The subjective aspect of culture (the beliefs, values, and explanatory cognitive frameworks, communicated verbally and nonverbally) is learned through social interaction in the family and in the general social milieu in which we live. The subjective properties of a culture have a pervasive impact on everything we see and do, and yet they remain largely invisible.

Culture underlies our beliefs, our values, and our behavior. Yet the magnitude of its pervasive character goes largely unremarked and unrecognized by most of us. Geert Hofstede refers to this property of culture metaphorically as the "software of the mind" (1990), drawing on people's computer experience to convey in a more concrete and palpable way the pervasive yet invisible influence of culture on our thought and behavior. Likewise, Edward and Mildred Hall approach their description of culture through simile: "Culture can be likened to an enormous, subtle, extraordinarily complex computer. It programs the actions and responses of every person, and these responses must be mastered by anyone wishing to make the system work" (Hall & Hall, 1987, pp. 3–4).

Culture, however, is also objective, in patterned behavior. In Bordieu's description, for example, of the implicit patterns of subjective experience (called "habitus"), the intersection of objective and subjective are apparent: "The habits of practical mastery [habitus] . . . are not perceived by actors as arbitrary or the product of successive habituating experiences but as natural and self-evident. . . . Subjective experience is a pattern of organization. . . . It is habituation to an unspoken rationale, inarticulate yet compelling because it is embodied in social interaction" (Partridge, 1987, p. 222).

Culture as Multileveled and Dynamic

Culture also needs to be thought of as operating on *several levels simultaneously*. It exists at the *micro level* of the individual—in a person's values, beliefs, explanatory systems, and behaviors, which are learned in the family and other basic social groups. Culture, however, also exists at the *macro level* in organizations and institutions encompassing schools, workplaces, media, government, the criminal justice system, and the like. The policies, procedures, and programs of these organizations and institutions embody the culture in which and through which we live.

It is organizations and their culture that frame our daily lives as individuals. They provide the generative matrix for our decisions and actions as individuals. Culture is *dynamic* in that it operates through us as individuals within these specific organizational contexts. Our daily decisions and behavior as individuals are the generative source of culture. Think, for instance, of how and why norms are implemented and changed, or of the way policies, procedures, and programs are interpreted and enacted: these processes are the generative source of culture. To quote applied anthropologist William Partridge (1987, p. 220):

> In this view, culture is not a driving determinative force as much as it is a product of ongoing social interaction. It is only one resource, upon which actors draw in an ever-present process of recasting, reinterpreting, reinventing and revising culture so that it conforms to the needs of social practice then emerging. . . . The result of this ever-present process of revision is the objective element of practice, and it exists as the product of prior social actions. Practical activity, then, is the generative act of cultural construction.

Discussing these properties of culture (multileveled and dynamic) helps in the recognition that culture is both inside and outside of us. It helps us also recognize that although each of us has assimilated our culture in the context of our social environment, the culture itself is shaped and perpetuated through our individual behavior and choices (Levinson, Foley, & Holland, 1996). In 1993, for example, the National Endowment for the Humanities (NEH) initiated a program entitled "A National Conversation on American Pluralism and Identity." The purpose of the program was to articulate perspectives on what it means to be an American. One of the outcomes of this program was the funding by NEH of a series of panel conversations at the Field Museum in Chicago. In seeking to translate to the public an approach to culture and diversity in its fullest sense, the forum focused on "how values arise, shape our actions and are continually re-shaped by our social interactions." The participants, furthermore, were presented with "the artificiality of cultural boundaries," and how we "choose social identities, including being attentive to the potency of concepts such as 'race' and 'ethnicity,' which we use in identifying ourselves" (Wali & Kahn, 1997).

Clearly, therefore, we each enjoy the power, through reflection and a fuller understanding of our culture, to *change it* in the daily choices we make and the way we interact with others.

Worksheet 2

Experiencing the Concept of Culture: The F-Perception Activity (approx. total time 20 mins.)

Purpose To demonstrate the concept of culture or "culture concept."

Instructions Your instructor will give you the *F*'s statement and will ask how many *F*s you see on first reading the statement. You could respond out loud and record the responses on the board. Discuss these initial responses.

Explanation It is significant that the statement is in English, since language is an aspect of culture. English as a language influences the reader here to select from the incoming information the smaller connecting words (*of, the,* and so forth) and to focus on the larger meaningful units (verbs, nouns, and so on). For this reason, most people see only about eight *F*s when they first read the statement. English here works as a kind of culture filter leading the reader unwittingly to exclude or "select out" things that are the very object of the reading. The point is that incoming information is filtered by beliefs and thoughts, which are culturally constructed, learned, and reinforced in daily social life.

Debriefing Questions

Write your answers to the debriefing questions in the spaces that follow.

1. Describe your personal reaction when you "saw" the ten f's.

2. What did you learn about yourself from this activity?

3. What did you learn about others?

4. Name two ways you can use this learning in daily life.

Worksheet 3

Experiencing the Concept of Culture: Shodop Culture (approx. total time 35 mins.)

Purpose To demonstrate the concept of culture or "culture concept."

Instructions Divide the class into two groups: the host culture and the visiting culture. Ask the visitors to leave the room, telling them you will meet with them momentarily to give them their instructions. Explain the rules of Shodop culture, as presented in the Instructor's Manual, to the host group. Answer any questions that arise. Next, meet with the visiting culture group and discuss their required tasks and clarify any questions. Finally, bring the groups together for interaction according to their respective roles. (approx. 20 mins.)

Debriefing Questions

Write your answers to the debriefing questions in the spaces that follow. (approx. 15 mins.)

1. Describe your personal reactions to Shodop culture.

2. Visitors, what do you think are the rules of Shodop culture?

3. What did you learn about yourself?

4. What did you learn about others?

5. Name two ways you can use this learning in daily life.

Aspects of Culture and Ethnicity

The following list of twelve aspects of culture and ethnicity is designed to work as a tool for observing and thinking about culture in general (the learned and shared way of life all humans possess) and the specific cultures we encounter at work and in other settings. The list provides a vocabulary for perceiving and discussing cultural differences and for obtaining relevant information in order to identify and solve problems (Hogan-Garcia & Wright, 1989). By "culture in general" (also called "cultural universals"), I mean the customary ways of living that all human groups enjoy, encompassing things like diet, family form, social-group organization, and religion. Set up thus as a list, the following "aspects" describe broad human culture. This list is "holistic" in this sense of inclusive. The list also provides a basis for discussing the beliefs and customs of specific cultures, such as the Mexican or the Vietnamese. The term *ethnic group* or *ethnicity* refers to the cultural heritage or aspects of culture that a group shares and that are learned from one generation by another. Ethnic groups maintain their cultural differences by means of isolating mechanisms such as geographic and social barriers. That is, the aspects of the group's culture (such as beliefs, identities, and boundaries) are set by the members *and* by pressures from outsiders (Montagu, 1974, p. 72).

1. *History:* The immigration or migration experience of a person or a group; the time period during which members of a group immigrated to the United States and the conditions of their immigration or migration.

2. *Social group interaction patterns:*
   - *Intragroup:* Relations among members *within* a group. Relations are influenced by age, gender, color, socioeconomic background, religion, education, language or dialect spoken, and acculturation processes, which includes culture shock.
   - *Intergroup:* Relations between members of *different* groups. Are they cooperative and friendly, or conflict ridden? Is there stereotyping and discrimination? Social status and social distance between groups is relevant here.

3. *Social status factors:* One's social position in society in relation to education, occupation, and income. (This aspect assumes economic, political [social control], education, and other institutions of nation states.)

4. *Value orientations:* The deep subjective ideals and standards by which members of a culture (or ethnic group) judge their personal actions or those of others.

5. *Language and communication:*
   - *Verbal:* Language, which provides the verbal categories for the perception of reality and for communication among humans.
   - *Nonverbal:* Tone of voice, gestures, facial expression, touching, body smell, and time orientation, which conveys meaning directly without the use of words. However subtle, nonverbal communication is a potent factor in culturally and socially diverse settings and gives rise to much misunderstanding.

6. *Family life processes:*
   - Gender roles
   - Occupations
   - Education
   - Marriage customs
   - Divorce practices (if practiced)
   - Parenting beliefs and practices

7. *Healing beliefs and practices:* The attitudes, beliefs and practices people have
   - toward health
   - toward the body
   - toward the determinants of disease
   - toward health practices
   - toward pain
   - toward death

8. *Religion:* Spiritual beliefs and practices.

9. *Art and expressive forms:* The creative use of imagination in interpreting, understanding, and enjoying life. Includes visual art, verbal art, and music.

10. *Diet:* The preferred foods eaten by members and their groups.

11. *Recreation:* Pastimes and activities for leisure and enjoyment.

12. *Clothes:* The types, style, and extent of body covering.

Worksheet 4

Aspects of Culture/Ethnicity (approx. total time 20 mins.)

Purpose To practice thinking about the specific aspects or properties of culture.

Instructions Form groups of two to four people and, using the list on pp. 19–20, discuss examples of any three aspects of culture that you have observed within the last two days. Someone in the group needs to write the examples on paper and someone else needs to report the examples to the whole group during the debriefing. (approx. 10 mins.)

Debriefing Questions

Write your answers to the debriefing questions in the spaces that follow. (approx. 10 mins.)

1. Describe your personal reaction (feelings and thoughts) in discussing the three aspects listed by your group.

2. What did you learn about yourself?

3. What did you learn about others?

4. Name two ways you can use what you have learned in your daily life.

Personal Culture

Personal culture (also called core identity) consists of the entirety of an individual's personal meaning system: beliefs, values, perceptions, assumptions, and explanatory frameworks about reality. It also includes the individual's unique constellation of usual behavior. One's personal culture develops in and through social interaction with family and other people in the sociocultural milieu. Ethnicity is one aspect of personal identity. Other aspects include age, race, gender, ableness, religion, physical appearance, sexual orientation, and social economic position. As a person's sociocultural milieu typically changes over the course of a lifetime, so does one's personal identity. It is this dynamic *entirety* that underlies individual behavior.

Worksheet 5

Personal Culture, Part 1 (approx. total time 20 mins.)

Purpose To provide an experience of one's personal culture.

Instructions For two or three minutes think about the following question: What is important to me in my daily life? Next, on a separate sheet of paper try to draw the images or ideas that came into your mind. Use stick figures, cartoons, or any other symbols that work for you. (approx. 10 mins.)

Debriefing Questions

Write your answers to the debriefing questions in the spaces that follow. (approx. 10 mins.)

1. Describe your feelings and thoughts as you attempted to portray your perception of your personal culture.

2. What did you learn about yourself in the course of this exercise?

*Adapted from the *Handbook for Developing Multicultural Awareness* by Paul Pedersen, 1988. Alexandria, VA: American Association for Counseling and Development.

3. What did you learn about others in the course of this exercise?

4. Name two ways in which you can use what you have learned in daily life.

Worksheet 6

Personal Culture, Part 2 (approx. total time 20 mins.)

Purpose To demonstrate aspects of personal culture.

Instructions From the list on pages 19–20, choose three aspects of culture and for each write an example of how this aspect is realized in your daily life. (approx. 10 mins.)

Example: As an example of family life processes, I live in an extended family, which is a source of both support and strain. My family structure provides me with ongoing support in the form of continuous, dense, and intimate communication across eleven households. It also provides all members with ready access to important resources: financial, emotional, and the like. At the same time, however, common knowledge of one another's life challenges can be a source of stress and strain because each person's struggle is in some way everyone's. At another cultural level, my life as a member of an extended family is counter to the norm of our national or mainstream culture. Mainstream U.S. culture is nuclear in structure (comprised of father, mother, and children, in one household) and it espouses an ethos of autonomy ("pull oneself up by one's own bootstraps") and self-reliance ("move out at eighteen"), as opposed to lifelong interdependency in my extended family.

Debriefing Questions

Write your answers to the debriefing questions in the spaces that follow. (approx. 10 mins.)

1. Describe your personal reaction (feelings, thoughts) to applying the three aspects to your personal culture.

2. What did you learn about yourself in the course of this exercise?

3. What did you learn about others in the course of this exercise?

4. Name two ways in which you can use what you have learned in daily life.

Culture or Ethnic Groups

A culture or ethnic group (the terms can be used interchangeably) is one in which the members share a common cultural heritage. This cultural heritage is a complex and dynamic reality made up of the values, beliefs, attitudes, and customs that relate to the aspects of culture we have been considering—for example, language, religion, and family life processes. Each of these aspects involve and operate through associated values, beliefs, assumptions, and customary behaviors. In this way, culture or ethnic groups represent associated belief and behavior systems and are passed on through learning and assimilation from one generation to the next. The beliefs and identities of members of an ethnic group are determined by its members and by pressures from outsiders. This is the process of survival for the culture or ethnic group.

With the exception of American Indians and African Americans, the United States is a "nation of immigrants." This means that each of us is to some extent a member of a culture or ethnic group. This is so even if we do not personally identify with that membership. The extent to which we identify with membership in a culture or ethnic group varies according to a variety of circumstances—for example, how many generations our family has been in the United States, whether we live in an ethnic or cultural community, and the frequency with which we interact with members of our cultural or ethnic community (Spector, 1996).

Worksheet 7

Culture or Ethnic Group (approx. total time 20 mins.)

Purpose To demonstrate group-level aspects of culture.

Instructions From the list on pages 19–20, choose three aspects of culture to apply to your experience of culture or ethnic group. For each, write an example of how this aspect is realized in your daily life. (approx. 10 mins.)

Example: As an example of history, my family of origin is Irish Catholic on my father's side. His maternal great grandfather and grandmother immigrated to Illinois from County Kilkinney during the Great Famine of 1846–49. I am commonly reminded of my Irish origins by the stories told at family gatherings.

Debriefing Questions

Write your answers to the debriefing questions in the spaces that follow. (approx. 10 mins.)

1. Describe your personal reaction (feelings, thoughts) to applying the three aspects to your experience of culture/ethnic group.

2. What did you learn about yourself in the course of this exercise?

3. What did you learn about others in the course of this exercise?

4. Name two ways in which you can use what you have learned in daily life.

Mainstream/National Culture

As a society, the United States is composed of a mainstream or national culture and many subcultures. We can name these subcultures: for example, Mexican-American, Irish-American, African-American, or Jewish-American. National or mainstream culture has at its base a core culture that is *English* in its origins and development. Mainstream or national culture, nevertheless, has developed its own distinctive and unique expressions of the twelve general aspects of culture we have been studying. (See Appendix A, "Aspects of the Mainstream U.S. Culture," for a list of these.) We often refer to mainstream or national culture as the dominant culture because it is incorporated in and informs all the major organizations and institutions of the United States. In this sense, we say that the dominant culture is *institutionalized* in our societal structures, being "hegemonic" (Nader, 1994, 1996). In this sense, too, we can say that the national or mainstream culture *presides* over all the various subcultures. What this means is that each of us must know how to recognize and "discourse" with this dominant culture in order to live and work comfortably in it, regardless of the culture or ethnic group to which we may otherwise belong (Levinson, Foley, & Holland, 1996; Sleeter & McLaren, 1995).

Worksheet 8

Mainstream/National U.S. Culture, Part 1

(approx. total time 10 mins.)

Instructions Read the characteristics of m-time and p-time in the table on page 36. Cite one example of m-time and one example of p-time you have witnessed. M-time is the prevailing time orientation of mainstream culture (Hall & Hall, 1987). (approx. 10 mins.)

Example: The m-time orientation operates in most institutions of the United States, such as the educational system.

Monochronic or M-Time	Polychronic or P-Time
Schedules and deadlines are very important: There is an urgency to maintain schedules.	Schedules are a goal, but personal commitments are more important and can disrupt one's schedule.
It is important to follow "the plan" ("set in stone").	Plans are flexible, perceived as guidelines, and are subject to change.
Promptness and being on time are very important.	Promptness is a goal, but personal commitments are more important, except in emergencies.
One does one activity at a time, concentrating on the job with no interruptions.	One does several activities at one time: jobs entail multiple tasks and many interruptions.
Direct verbal communication is relied upon (low context: situational factors are not perceived as important for communicating meaning).	Verbal and nonverbal communication are relied upon (high context: status and other situational factors communicate meaning).
Commitment to one's job is highly valued.	Commitment to relationships is more important than one's job.
Private property is greatly valued (there is a reluctance to lend or borrow).	Private property is not valued over relationships; property is often lent, given away, and borrowed.
Consideration for one's and others' privacy is important.	Continuous and close interactions with family and friends is more important than privacy.
Casual, short-term relationships are acceptable.	Casual, short-term relationships are perceived as superficial.

Worksheet 9

Mainstream/National U.S. Culture, Part 2

(approx. total time 20 mins.)

Purpose To demonstrate aspects of mainstream U.S. culture.

Instructions Form groups of four to five persons and discuss any three of the general aspects of culture (see the list on pages 19–20) as they relate to mainstream or national U.S. culture. For each aspect you select, write an example of how it is realized in life as you have experienced it. (approx. 10 mins.)

Debriefing Questions

Write your answers to the debriefing questions in the following spaces.
(approx. 10 mins.)

1. Describe your personal reaction (feelings, thoughts) to applying the
   three aspects to your experience of mainstream/national U.S.
   culture.

2. What did you learn about yourself in the course of this exercise?

3. What did you learn about others in the course of this exercise?

4. Name two ways in which you can use what you have learned in
   daily life.

Organizational Culture

Organizational culture refers to the policies, procedures, programs, and processes that organizations or institutions employ. Within each of these organizational policies, procedures, programs, and processes we find deeply embedded values, beliefs, assumptions, and customary ways of behaving (Hamada & Sibley, 1994; Jordan, 1994; Wright, 1994). And we can isolate and examine these various factors in organizational policies, procedures, and all the rest. It is important here also to recognize that organizational culture in the United States is highly *congruent* with mainstream or national culture—it reflects and echoes mainstream culture in virtually every respect. The institutionalization of monochronic time orientation, perception, and use of time are good examples of this congruence of organizational and mainstream culture.

Worksheet 10

Organizational Culture (approx. total time 20 mins.)

Purpose To demonstrate aspects of organizational culture.

Instructions Form groups of four to five persons and discuss any three of the general aspects of culture (see the list on pages 19–20) as they relate to organizational culture in the United States. For each aspect you select, write an example of how it is realized in life as you have experienced it. (approx. 10 mins.)

Example: The institutionalization of monochronic time orientation, perception, and use of time are good examples of this congruence of organizational and mainstream culture.

Debriefing Questions

Write your answers to the debriefing questions in the following spaces. (approx. 10 mins.)

1. Describe your personal reaction (feelings, thoughts) to applying the three aspects to your experience of organizational culture in the United States.

2. What did you learn about yourself in the course of this exercise?

3. What did you learn about others in the course of this exercise?

4. Name two ways in which you can use what you have learned in daily life.

In Chapter 2 we have defined and worked with skill 1: understanding culture as it operates on different social levels. In Chapter 3 we will do the same with skill 2: understanding common barriers to effective communication and relationships.

Chapter 3

Skill Two

Understanding Common Barriers to Effective Communication and Relationships

Similar to skill 1, skill 2 fosters cultural awareness and understanding, collectively called culture-mindedness. Persons who are culture-minded recognize different ways of thinking and communicating, and they watch the texture of relations closely. Culture-minded persons in any situation attend closely to the demeanor and behavior of people around them in their interaction. At another level, they are also sensitive to the treatment style of the organization. Whereas skill 1 focuses on cultural dimensions (that is, the twelve general aspects of culture) and levels of complexity (personal, culture group, mainstream/national, and organizational), skill 2 focuses on six barriers to effective communication and relationships (Pederson, 1988, pp. 23–25). A list of these six barriers provides a conceptual tool for recognizing and understanding the cultural dynamics at play in group patterns of social interaction, especially when cultural understanding—culture-mindedness—is lacking. The six barriers divide conveniently into two broad types based on levels of complexity: the interpersonal level and the organizational/systems level.

Personal and interpersonal barriers:

1. language
2. nonverbal communication
3. preconceptions, stereotypes, and discrimination
4. judgments
5. stress

Organizationwide barriers:

6. organization policies, procedures, and programs unfriendly to cultural diversity

Personal and Interpersonal Barriers

Five barriers operate interpersonally to negatively influence communication and relationships with people of diverse cultures. These barriers are as follows:

1. language
2. nonverbal communication
3. preconceptions, stereotypes, and discrimination
4. judgment
5. stress

Language refers to the system of verbal communication that was defined previously in my description of the general aspects of culture and ethnicity. Similarly, *nonverbal communication* (things such as body stance, body smell, gestures, eye contact) has been defined previously under the general aspects of culture. *Preconceptions and stereotypes* function as negative lenses through which one perceives people who look and act differently. Such preconceptions and stereotypes are usually based on overgeneralized beliefs, assumptions, and misinformation. *Discriminatory treatment* is a natural consequence of the distorted view that results from preconceived and stereotypical thinking, because the negative assumptions and beliefs provide psychological permission to behave in a way that discriminates against difference perceived in others. The prevailing stereotypes and discrimination center on what some researchers call the "isms": racism, sexism, classism, ageism, and homophobia (Delgado & Stefancic, 1997; Essed, 1991; Sleeter & McLaren, 1995; Stewart & Bennet, 1991; Tatum, 1993, 1997).

Related to preconceptions, stereotypes, and discrimination is the *judgment* barrier. This barrier is an unconscious and automatic tendency to pass negative judgment on people who look and behave in unfamiliar ways. The negative judgment may derive from *ethnocentrism*. Ethnocentrism is a common human tendency to judge others by one's own cultural values and standards, which are perceived as superior (Ferraro, 1990; Lett, 1987). Although equality and social justice are foundation principles of mainstream culture, there is also the tradition of intolerance for diversity, such as nativism, a subject to which I turn in the section on organizationwide barriers.

Situations in which familiar communication and behavioral cues are missing usually give rise to stress, the fifth barrier. The anxiety that is the product of these situations is what we mean here by the *stress barrier* (Brislen, 1986, pp. 241–266; Hall & Hall, 1987; Sikkema & Niyekawa, 1987, pp. 6–9). And this stress barrier can and often does affect all parties. For members of minority groups (Blacks, Asians, women, gays, and so on), more specifically, stress can stem from being treated as an "open person"—one who is a special target of hostile treatment because she or he is perceived as different and therefore deserving of contempt (Feagin, 1991). It is useful to think of stress as layered. General stress is experienced by most people in relation to such issues as health, family, work, school, and finances. For people of minority status there are additional stressors, such as invisibility, social exclusion, unrelenting pressure to prove oneself, denial of one's experience, as well even as verbal and physical harassment or assault. In addition, people who are immigrants commonly experience the stress of culture shock (when the cues and fabric of daily life are totally different) as well as the pressure to hurry up and learn mainstream culture's language, values, and lifeways (acculturation stress) (Padilla, 1986).

Worksheet 11

Barriers to Communication: Cross-Cultural Speaking

(approx. total time 30 mins.)

Purpose To foster awareness and understanding of the verbal and nonverbal barriers to communication in a culturally diverse context.

Instructions Form four groups, named 1, 2, 3, and 4. Your instructor will hand your group a set of instructions. Read and become familiar with your group's instructions. Then pair off with someone from another group and, following your instructions, learn three points of information about the other person. (approx. 20 mins.)

Debriefing Questions

Write your answers to the debriefing questions in the following spaces. (approx. 10 mins.)

1. Describe your personal reaction (feelings, thoughts) to the role-playing exercise as applied to the verbal and nonverbal barriers to effective communication and relationships that can arise in a culturally diverse context. Did you experience any of the other barriers?

2. Ask one person from each of the four groups to read his or her instructions aloud before the whole group.

3. What did you learn about yourself in the course of this exercise?

4. What did you learn about others in the course of this exercise?

5. Name two ways in which you can use what you have learned in daily life.

Worksheet 12

Barriers to Communication: Case of the Green-Haired People (approx. total time 30 mins.)

Purpose To foster awareness and understanding of the barriers to effective communication and relationships in culturally diverse settings.

Instructions Read the following extract, "The Case of The Green Haired People." (approx. 20 mins.)

The Case of the People with Green Hair*

John Doe is not born with prejudice against other human beings who have green hair. But from the time he is a tiny tot, John Doe is warned against them. Don't play with the children with green hair. Don't talk to them. Stay with your own kind. You're a bad boy, John Doe, if you have anything to do with the green-haired children. John Doe learns not only from his parents' words but also from tone of voice, facial expressions, and gestures.

As John grows older, he learns that his parents and their friends and neighbors do not want people with green hair to attend his church, to live in his neighborhood, to go to his school, or playground, or camp. The adults who control John's life, and whom he imitates and depends upon, insist that the people with green hair stay in their place. Everybody with whom little John Doe is acquainted believes that green-haired people should worship elsewhere, live elsewhere, and be educated elsewhere. As a child, John Doe very seldom even sees people with green hair.

As to jobs, the family of little John Doe believes that people with green hair should do the heavy and the dirty work which people like John Doe's folks need done but don't want to do themselves. The better jobs, in professions or businesses, should belong to people like John's father and mother. If people with green hair do hold any such job, they should be restricted to working for their own kind, the people with green hair.

The people with green hair whom John does encounter are those who do the heavy and the dirty jobs for his family. Naturally, these folks do not happen to be the more able green-haired people. Instead, they are the people who can obtain only this type of work. They are not well educated. They dress poorly. They get dirty on the job. So John Doe's first actual childhood experience with the people with green

*Prejudiced—How Do People Get That Way? William Van Til, pp. 10–12. Reprinted with permission of Anti-Defamation League of B'nai B'rith, Tenth printing, 1975.

hair help persuade him that his family is right. Green-haired people, he can plainly see, are inferior people. They are uneducated, poor, dirty.

The way things are, there can be almost no communication between John Doe and the people with green hair. John has no reliable way of telling what green-haired people are thinking. True, he occasionally reads about people with green hair in his local newspaper. But, since conflict makes news, his newspaper usually reports on people with green hair who happen to get themselves into trouble with the law. When the name of a person with green hair appears in the news, the local newspaper carefully places the words "green hair" after the individual's name. John often comes away from his newspaper with the clear impression that too many green-haired people get themselves into difficult situations. The conclusion that everything has conspired to teach him since infancy becomes more confirmed. People with green hair are people who do bad things. Even the newspapers say so.

Since he has no way of communicating directly with people who have green hair, John Doe is an easy prey for wild rumors concerning "greenies," as many contemptuously call them. John hears that "greenies" want to marry people with "superior" hair color and thus make everybody's hair partly green. Though people with green hair repeatedly deny this rumor and plaintively explain that all they want is to be treated like human beings, John clutches on to the rumor. It strengthens his resolve to keep people with green hair in their place so that people like himself and his family will not be forced to live at the low level at which the people with green hair are forced to live.

Time moves along. John Doe becomes a man. He follows the patterns he has learned. He marries Jane Doe, who has learned the same prejudices against people with green hair. Eventually, they become parents. And what do they teach their children? "Don't play with the children with green hair. You are bad if you do."

John Doe has learned to be prejudiced against people with green hair. How did John get that way? The total environment in which John Doe lived encouraged prejudice against people with green hair. He learned his prejudices from his parents, their friends, and his neighbors. He learned them from his limited observations. He learned them from his reading of his newspaper. He learned them from his separation from green-haired people on his job. He developed an unattractive picture in his mind, an ugly stereotype of people with green hair. So, in turn, John Doe carried over his prejudices to his children. Because they noticed and imitated their father's feelings, John Doe's children, too, became infected with the disease called prejudice.

Nothing ever broke the circle that closed John Doe in with his prejudices against people with green hair. Things were so arranged by John Doe's family that he found himself walled in by the circle almost from birth. In turn, John Doe began to build a circle of prejudice around his own children from the time of their birth.

Debriefing Questions

Write your answers to the debriefing questions in the following spaces. (approx. 10 mins.)

1. Describe your personal reaction (feelings, thoughts) to reading and discussing the case example.

2. How many barriers are evident in the case of the green-haired people?

3. What did you learn about yourself in the course of this exercise?

4. What did you learn about others in the course of this exercise?

5. Name two ways in which you can use what you have learned in daily life.

Organizationwide Barriers

Organizationwide barriers are the second broad category of barriers to effective communication and relationships. Organizational policies, procedures, and programs set the context for employee relations. These policies, procedures, and programs become the sixth barrier when they support disrespectful, unequal, and inequitable relationships among employees. The cultural assumptions embedded in these organizational policies, procedures, and programs are highly congruent with the assumptions of mainstream culture (Hamada & Sibley, 1994; Schwartzman, 1993; Walck & Jordan, 1995; Wright, 1994).

Five Assumptions about Cultural Diversity

Five themes or assumptions of mainstream culture (Kohls, 1984; Tatum, 1992) in relation to diversity are significant and especially noteworthy here, given their influence in fostering the cultural-diversity barriers:

1. The United States is a meritocracy.
2. Americans don't have a culture.
3. If it is different, it is wrong.
4. One should never talk about cultural diversity.
5. One should never admit to being prejudiced.

The first assumption, that *the United States is a meritocracy,* is a common theme we have all met in the socialization process in the United States. Schools and media, two powerful agents of socialization, regularly project U.S. institutions as "color-blind" and as presenting to all participants a "level playing field." For this reason, if an individual does not succeed, it is assumed that it is as a result of laziness, negligence, or some other personal fault, since by definition the social system is assumed to be fair (McIntosh, 1993). Lack of success is regularly construed as proceeding from the individual's failure, rather than the failure of society to develop opportunity structures viable for all concerned and not just for the members of elite groups (Fine, 1990). It is clear that the national or mainstream culture's core values of individual autonomy and self-determination provide ideological support for the belief in a supposed meritocracy (Rose, 1990; Stewart & Bennet, 1991).

The second assumption, *Americans don't have a culture*, also derives from the emphasis on individual autonomy and self-determination in the United States: Americans don't have a culture because Americans are autonomous decision-makers who create their individualized way of living (Kohls, 1984). Clearly, we move in the land of myth and fantasy here, but on the operational level of day-to-day life such assumptions are experienced as virtually normative.

If it's different, it's wrong is the third assumption that operates in the national culture of the United States. At times in our history this assumption has been referred to as racism and gives rise to some of the "anti's" with which most of us are familiar: anti-Semitic, anti-immigrant, anti-Catholic, anti-non-White. A major support for racism is the strong popular belief in races as distinct biological entities, although science rejects the concept because human variation is continuous, not discreet (Montagu 1974; Leiberman & Rice 1997). The popular belief in the race concept derives from the world view of Europeans, dating back to at least 1600. As the Europeans built overseas empires in the Americas, Asia, and Africa, the race concept fostered support for the decimation and impoverishment of the peoples of these continents. The idea of the existence of distinct races and the inferiority of the non-European races grew over time, being socially constructed by these historical events. The history of the concept in the United States depicts the entire world as divided into three distinct races: Negroid, Caucasoid, and Asian. These three races are described on the basis of observable physical features: skin color, nasal width, hair texture, eye shape. The stereotype of "the three big races" has become so prevalent that they are viewed "as true, natural and inescapable" (Leiberman, 1997, p. 2). Every individual is perceived as *having* to belong to one or more of these races. In the late nineteenth century, another development in racial ideology came to overlay "the three big races": European races were defined as comprised of the Nordic, Alpine, and Mediterranean races. Additionally, the belief that the Jews and the Irish were separate and debased races was added to the racial ideology.

Another dimension in the development of the racial ideology of the mainstream (national) culture of the United States is the cultural rule of hypodescent. The rule of hypodescent, or the "one-drop rule," defines a person as lower in status or position if that person has just *one* ancestor who was a member of a group lower in the society's group hierarchy. Thus, any person with an African-American, Mexican-American, or Native-American ancestor is socially defined and perceived as African American, Mexican American, or Native American, even though that person may identify with his Irish-American family of origin.

One should never talk about diversity, the fourth assumption of mainstream U.S. culture, is actually a subtle *behavioral assumption* enforced by a tacit belief in the national policy of "Anglo-conformity." For decades, the Anglo-conformity mentality has worked to implement the forced assimilation of culturally diverse groups, of which Native Americans and African slaves are only two clear examples (Feagin, 1996).

One should never admit to being prejudiced, the final cultural assumption on our list, is also age-old and equally tacit. Never admitting personal prejudice is a dynamic that works to curtail even the perception that one is prejudiced, let alone the analysis of institutional and systemic inequities, thus supporting the belief in meritocracy.

Stages of Sociocultural Awareness and Identity Change

A significant issue in the development of diversity competence is the degree to which one is aware of these assumptions of mainstream culture (the national culture of the United States) in the context of daily life. The construction of one's sense of self is heavily influenced by mainstream culture's monocultural assumptions and policies, as implemented, for example, in schools and the media. It is also heavily influenced by mainstream culture's mechanisms of stratification, which are based on these five assumptions. These mechanisms of stratification are ideological and institutionalized mechanisms for placing people on certain rungs of the societal ladder, rungs that determine their access to resources and therefore the quality of life they enjoy. And these stratifying mechanisms are activated and brought into play by many things outside one's control—one's ethnicity, gender, socioeconomic status, sexual orientation, ableness, and age (DeAnda, 1984; Essed, 1991; Helms, 1989; Phinney, 1989, 1990; Tatum, 1992, 1997). Mainstream culture's monocultural assumptions and stratification mechanisms thus profoundly affect the personality development of *all* those who live in this society, even though one may not be conscious of these effects. This means that we have all been schooled by mainstream American culture, through the organizations and institutions in which we live our lives, to think in a certain way about diversity. And this means in turn that most of us are struggling at stage 1 or 2 in the identity-change process, a subject to which I now turn.

It is not the purpose of this book to attempt a lengthy explanation of the identity-change process, a complex sociocultural and psychological phenomenon (Phinney & Rotherman, 1987; Root, 1992). Nevertheless, it is important to discuss the different stages of sociocultural awareness that occur in the identity-change process, because they manifest themselves in the interpersonal behaviors that arise in work domains and other settings. The dynamics of the different stages profoundly affect interpersonal relations by forming barriers to effective communication and relationships in culturally diverse settings.

Therefore, the topic of personal identity as regards personal awareness of mainstream cultural assumptions and social stratification is central to the development of cultural competence because it relates centrally to personal and interpersonal barriers (such as stereotypes, negative judgments, and stress). It is these barriers that currently give rise to the conflicts that occur in workplaces and communities and that make this training program pertinent and useful. Note, too, that these barriers spring from one's personal culture. For example, stereotyping and negative judgments flow from misinformation and the lack of cultural understanding (Tatum, 1992), clearly matters of personal culture.

The identity-change stages are integrally related to learning cultural diversity competence. One's identity consists of one's personal meanings, beliefs, and deep assumptions about reality—that is, one's personal paradigm. An identity change thus implies a change in one's personal paradigm. Consequently, when individuals engage in a training process designed to sensitize them to such barriers as stereotyping and negative judgment, they emphatically begin addressing their personal meanings, beliefs, and deep assumptions about reality. In this sense, identity change and social awareness are integrally involved in learning diversity competence (Gochenour, 1993; Paige, 1993).

Note, too, that identity awareness and change, like all organic changes, do not take place in the neat sequential order typical of the printed page or a visual aid. As an organic developmental process, identity change for cultural diversity competence is largely nonsequential, nonlinear. Participants can expect to find themselves taking two steps forward only to take one step back in the work of developing diversity competence. Finally, too, it is important to recognize in this connection that in learning diversity competence we often require new cultural information so that we can begin to perceive and think about cultural diversity in fresh, positive ways. Fresh cultural information makes it possible to neutralize the negative emotional reactions often attendant upon identity change as well as the experience of cultural change and diversity in general. Let us then briefly review identity change stages as they relate to sociocultural awareness.

Stage 1: Conformity Individuals at stage 1 do not recognize the impact that the meritocracy assumption or the denial of social stratification has on their lives. Preconceptions, stereotypes, confusion, stress, and denial or nonrecognition of sensitive issues related to diversity are the common characteristics of stage 1, the stage of conformity (Loden & Rosener, 1991; Morrison, 1992). Organizational policies, procedures, and programs support and perpetuate the conformity stage in individuals. School curriculums and programs that lack components about cultural diversity also perpetuate the stage of conformity by fostering a monocultural perception and inducing a blindness to the current and historical reality of cultural diversity (Delgado & Stefancic, 1997; Sleeter & McLaren, 1995). The remarks of Chris, a White man, when he viewed the first episode of the documentary "Eyes on the Prize," illustrates stage 1 nicely:

> I never knew it [racism] was really that bad just 35 years ago. Why didn't I learn this in elementary or high school? Could it be that White people want

to forget this injustice? . . . I will never forget that movie for as long as I live. It was like a big slap in the face. (Tatum, 1992, p. 7)

Stage 2: Resistance At stage 2, individuals question and resist anything that seems to contradict mainstream culture's assumptions and beliefs about diversity with which they have been socialized. Beverly Tatum again clearly illustrates the dynamics of stage 2 resistance in the case of a White woman who, when exposed to information about racist policy during World War II, "felt anger and embarrassment in response to her previous lack of information about the internment of the Japanese Americans" (Tatum, 1992, p. 7).

Stage 3: Redefinition Individuals at stage 3 characteristically begin to redefine their identity in terms of the growing awareness and sensitivity they are discovering in themselves as regards diversity and the impact they gradually come to see it has on their lives and those of others. At the end of a semester-long course on race, ethnic, and gender relations in America, students were asked to write about the effects of their coursework on them. The following selections from their responses illustrate aptly the redefinition stage of identity change:

> I never realized how much "our" history books left out as to our involvement in the colonizing of other cultures.

> My view that women had progressed greatly in the workplace in terms of discrimination and sexual harassment was changed.

> I was unaware until this semester that land and possessions of Japanese forced into concentration camps was not returned. It helped me understand why monetary compensation received by the Japanese several years ago was so important.

> The first racial paradigm of mine that was challenged was the continued harassment of Afro-Americans. I could not believe that this ethnic group still faces many obstacles in their path toward moving up in society. Another viewpoint of mine that was changed was the amount of sexual harassment in jobs and education. (Hogan-Garcia, Wright, & Corey, 1991, pp. 88–89)

Stage 4: New Identity Individuals at stage 4 have begun to feel comfortable with their new identity based on the awareness and understanding they have achieved of cultural and social diversity issues in the United States.

Stage 5: Diversity Competence At stage 5, individuals have achieved considerable growth in diversity competence and find themselves regularly and increasingly able to develop effective relationships with people technically described as culturally and socially diverse others (DeAnda, 1984; Foster et al., 1988; Helms, 1989; Sue, 1981; Tatum, 1992).

Worksheet 13

Barriers to Communication: Case Analysis, Part 1 (approx. total time 30 mins.)

Purpose To foster awareness and understanding of the six common barriers to communication and congenial relationships in culturally diverse contexts.

Instructions Form groups of four to five people and describe in the space below a cultural diversity issue or conflict occurring in any setting within the last year. It might be an incident you experienced personally or one you heard about. Try to be alert to the five cultural assumptions that are so prevalent in U.S. life. Try also to include such elements of diversity as gender, ethnicity, race, age, and socioeconomic status. Feel free to frame your discussion from any number of points of view and roles: as a supervisor or subordinate in a supervisory relationship, for example; or as a teacher or student in a teacher-student relationship; or as a co-worker in a co-worker relationship. Discuss and identify the operative barriers. (approx. 15 mins.)

Example: I was employed as an attorney at a law firm and one of my duties was to conduct initial interviews of prospective clients to determine if they had a viable case. A Chinese man was ushered into my office and I introduced myself as the attorney who would be interviewing him. He stopped dead and expressed great surprise and consternation at being interviewed by a woman. He said he had expected to see a man and asked if there was a man available. I told him I was the only person there but I could direct him to another office if he felt uncomfortable talking to me. He said he needed to think about it so I explained my background to him while he was pondering. He finally agreed to stay and suddenly turned very respectful. He insisted on calling me "Doctor" even after I explained to him that attorneys are not usually called Doctor.

Debriefing Questions

Write your answers to the debriefing questions in the following spaces. (approx. 15 mins.)

1. Describe your personal reaction (feelings, thoughts) to the discussion and case analysis in relation to the six common barriers.

2. What did you learn about yourself in the course of this exercise?

3. What did you learn about others in the course of this exercise?

4. Name two ways in which you can use what you have learned in daily life.

Worksheet 14

Barriers to Communication: Case Analysis, Part 2 (approx. total time 30 mins.)

Purpose To foster awareness and understanding of organizational and institutionwide barriers to effective communication and relationships in culturally diverse contexts.

Instructions Form groups of four to five people and describe in the space below a cultural diversity issue or conflict occurring in a work setting within the last year. It might be an incident you experienced personally or one you heard about. It may include such elements of diversity as gender, ethnicity, race, age, socioeconomic status, or sexual orientation. Feel free to frame your discussion from any number of points of view and roles: as a supervisor or subordinate in a supervisory relationship, for example; or as a teacher or student in a teacher-student relationship; or as a co-worker in a co-worker relationship. Discuss the specific barriers you can isolate in the case example you describe; list these barriers and cite specific concrete examples. Then regroup with the class to discuss the case examples and analyses produced in each of the small groups. (approx. 15 mins.)

Example: In a large civic organization, a Hispanic family entered through the wrong door and were automatically sent to the "court referral program" without being asked which department they were seeking and in a tone that made them feel "accused of something." Later it was found that one member of the family was attempting to join the organization as a volunteer, had an appointment, and was expected. The tone then changed to one of welcome.

Barriers include stereotyping, verbal communication (tone), nonverbal communication (body language), judgment, and stress. Organizationwide barriers exist if any of the five cultural assumptions can be isolated and especially if there is a pattern of practice (if such cases are common enough to become a pattern).

Debriefing Questions

Write your answers to the debriefing questions in the following spaces. (approx. 15 mins.)

1. Describe your personal reaction (feelings, thoughts) to the foregoing exercise.

2. What did you learn about yourself in the course of this exercise?

3. What did you learn about others in the course of this exercise?

4. Name two ways in which you can use what you have learned in daily life.

In Chapter 3 we have worked with the six barriers to effective communication and interpersonal relationships. In the next chapter we turn our attention to the personal and interpersonal cultural skills.

Chapter 4

Skill Three

Practicing Personal and Interpersonal Cultural Competence

The Personal Competencies

In this first part of Chapter 4, I set out a list of fourteen personal competencies for establishing effective relationships across cultural differences. I have isolated and refined these competencies from the work of various researchers and practitioners (Hogan-Garcia, 1994, 1995). The competencies are important individually and they are interrelated as well. Daily practice of the personal competencies, the daily work of making them your "personal culture," provides a personal foundation for engaging in the dialogue process of a culturally diverse environment.

The dialogue and conflict-recovery process are pivotal skills as well. These skills provide critical information about culturally diverse ways of thinking and acting, and in this way make effective interaction and communication in the culturally diverse environment possible. Without the reflective practice of the personal competencies as a foundation, the barriers will inevitably arise and the dialogue process will die. Without the dialogue process, conflict recovery and problem solving are usually impossible. Each part of the interpersonal process—dialogue, conflict recovery, and problem solving—hinges on the development of the following fourteen personal competencies, framed as mandates or directives:

1. Be nonjudgmental.
2. Be flexible.
3. Be resourceful.
4. Personalize observations.
5. Pay attention to your feelings.
6. Listen carefully.
7. Observe attentively.
8. Assume complexity.

9. Tolerate the stress of uncertainty.

10. Have patience.

11. Manage personal biases and stereotypes.

12. Keep a sense of humor.

13. Show respect.

14. Show empathy.

This list of fourteen cultural competencies can be viewed as the "Fourteen Commandments" of the culturally competent person. Let us review each in turn.

1. To *be nonjudgmental* means to short-circuit, unplug, or otherwise shut down the common tendency to negatively judge others perceived as different. To judge negatively means to cast the other person in an unfavorable light, to view the other person with disfavor.

2. To *be flexible* means to readjust quickly and effectively in quickly changing situations and to keep readjusting as often as necessary.

3. To *be resourceful* means skillfully and promptly to obtain the things required to respond effectively to a given situation.

4. To *personalize observations* means to express appropriately your personal feelings, thoughts, ideas, and beliefs in a warmly personal way— to deal with the other person on an individual basis as one fellow human being to another. This competency recognizes that one's personal perceptions, feelings, attitudes, and beliefs may *not* be shared by the other person. Three attendant skills (drawn from counseling practice; see, for example, Ivey & Gluckstern, 1982) help to personalize observations:

- *Communicate with "I-messages" rather than "you-messages":* Say, for example, "I disagree," rather than, "You're wrong."

- *Paraphrase* and in this way *repeat back* what you are hearing in conversation with the other person. For example: "Am I hearing you say that you want to reschedule our meeting?"

- *Listen actively:* Active listening calls for verbal indicators such as "uh-huh" or "yes" at regular intervals in the conversation. In this way you convey your close attention to the speaker.

5. To *pay attention to your feelings* means that you take your feelings seriously: you keep in touch with your interior reactions to the person with whom you are in conversation. Alert to your interior and secret responses, you can more easily and unerringly frame your verbal and nonverbal responses in an effective way. By paying attention to your feelings, you put yourself in better charge of yourself and in better command of the interpersonal situation.

6 and 7. To *listen carefully* and to *observe attentively* overlap with the active listening skill described above with respect to personalizing observations. Careful listening and attentive observation help increase sensitivity to the whole message—not just what is being said in words, but the message beyond the words and carried by such things as tone, body stance, and posture.

8. To *assume complexity* means to recognize in an ongoing way that in a culturally diverse environment, perspectives are multiple and possible outcomes are equally multiple.

9. To *tolerate the stress of uncertainty* means to avoid showing any irritation or annoyance you may be feeling with the ambiguity of the culturally diverse situation. This cultural competency overlaps with paying attention to your feelings (#5 above). Fear, anger, anxiety, and frustration are powerful forces when they are at work inside us, and they call for serious attention, especially in culturally diverse encounters.

10. To *have patience* is another effective and positive way to respond to stress. Here patience means the *practice* of preserving calm in challenging circumstances and of proceeding in a stable way and with persistence throughout the course of the trying situation.

11. To *manage personal biases* means that you always move beyond your personal outlook and point of view so that you treat the person before you as an individual, in full acknowledgment that no one person ever typifies a group.

12. To *keep a sense of humor* means to cultivate an active awareness of the absurdity that often arises when differences converge and to avoid taking things so seriously that you lose your perspective and are unable to laugh at yourself and *with* others (never *at* others).

13. To *show respect* means to go out of your way to express in a genuine and authentic manner the understanding, honor, and esteem you cultivate for the person(s) with whom you are dealing.

14. To *show empathy* means to experience the other person's perspectives, feelings, beliefs, and attitudes as if they were your own. To "put yourself in the other person's shoes" is the old catch phrase. Empathy is critical in the culturally diverse encounter. One effective and enjoyable stratagem for enlarging empathy is an ongoing reading program focused on "minority" or "special interest" novels. There is a huge and ever-growing library of novels arising out of the Chicano/Chicana, Latin-American, African-American, Asian-American, feminist, and gay and lesbian experience, to name a few (Hogan-Garcia & Wright, 1989).

Worksheet 15

The Fourteen Personal Competencies for Effective Communication and Relationships (approx. total time 25 mins.)

Purpose To foster awareness and understanding of the fourteen personal competencies for maintaining effective communication and relationships in a culturally diverse context.

Instructions Form groups of four to five people. Using the two case examples you developed in Worksheets 13 and 14, discuss and identify any competencies that would *improve* the interactions in the case examples. In conclusion, present your analysis to the class. (approx. 15 mins.)

Debriefing Questions

Write your answers to the debriefing questions in the following spaces. (approx. 10 mins.)

1. Describe your personal reaction (feelings, thoughts) to the exercise as regards the cultural competencies that ensure effective communication and relationships amidst cultural diversity.

2. What did you learn about yourself in the course of this exercise?

3. What did you learn about others in the course of this exercise?

4. Name two ways in which you can use what you have learned in daily life.

The Dialogue Process

Dialogue is the exchange of information between people who are willing to listen to one another's perspective in order to comprehend the meaning. It is based on the premise of mutual respect and open inquiry. It does not involve proving one's own viewpoint is "right." In brief, the dialogue process proceeds in four steps:

1. The parties initiate the dialogue by establishing the ground rules of the procedure. They mutually determine what is and is not allowed.

2. The parties in dialogue listen without interruption and with undivided attention to the viewpoints of each party.

3. Each party restates what he or she thinks was heard. This step permits the parties to demonstrate that they were listening as well as what they actually heard. Points of misunderstanding or forgotten points come to the fore. This heads off further conflict and allows the parties to rephrase and refine their comments, observations, and viewpoints.

4. Each party gives voice to his or her viewpoint. This means that the parties give *full* expression to their thoughts and feelings about the subject of dialogue.

Of the four steps, step 4 is pivotal. In one project, for example, administrators of a school district wanted to improve relations with the parents of the African-American students in the district. To further this initiative, they convened a community forum to discuss the parents' issues and concerns. For one hour the hurt and angry parents took turns voicing their thoughts, feelings, and views. At this point in the forum the administrators did not follow up with a statement of their own views, nor did they describe the programs they were formulating to address the parents' concerns and to include the parents in the district's school policies. Having politely listened to the parents, the administrators simply closed the meeting.

From our description of the dialogue process, it is clear that with the omission of the pivotal fourth step, no dialogue took place between the African-American parents and the school administrators. For dialogue, all parties must participate in the discussion, freely, candidly, and honestly sharing their views. In the present example we can also see that given the magnitude of the parents' grievances, the administrators needed to give the dialogue process more time, scheduling several sessions and fostering the growth of a close working relationship between administrators and parents.

The Conflict-Recovery Process

Awareness and practice of recovery skills are needed for reestablishing rapport when mistakes and conflicts occur. The conflict-recovery process, like the dialogue process, proceeds in four steps:

1. The parties begin the conflict-recovery process by openly acknowledging the point of disagreement, misunderstanding, or hostility. They do this in a "proactive" manner—that is, with the clear intention of solving the point of difficulty and *not* merely of rehearsing grievances, fixing blame, or allotting punishment.

2. The parties engage in dialogue according to the process outlined earlier.

3. The parties agree to work with a mediator or culture broker, if necessary, to come to some kind of agreement or make progress in exploring their dispute. (In the case of the administrators versus the African-American parents, for example, I suggested the parties engage a mediator in order to reestablish trust and initiate renewed dialogue.)

4. The parties discuss whatever options they can devise for reducing conflict, and they work out a plan of action with designated tasks and a suitable timetable agreeable to all parties.

From these remarks it should be clear that the conflict-recovery process envisioned here is a dynamic, ongoing series of initiatives that continually addresses the *sources* of conflict in a given group and works to bring about positive change in a *dynamic of change*. In this sense, conflict *resolution* may be an elusive and unrealistic goal, whereas the conflict management and conflict healing implied in the term *conflict recovery* may provide a more useful model to work from.

Worksheet 16

Two Communication Skills for Effective Dialogue (approx. total time 30 mins.)

Purpose To practice two communication skills that help integrate personal competencies into dialogues.

Instructions

1. *I-message vs. you-message.* Pair off with someone next to you. Devise a conversational scenario in which two people are talking. Then let each person take turns performing the scenario, employing first the you-message format and second the I-message format. (approx. 10 mins.)

   Example: Two colleagues are discussing directions to a meeting in another building. One colleague, visibly angry, yells: "YOU'RE WRONG!" [you-message] The other colleague replies: "I disagree. I think it's this way." [I-message]

2. *Paraphrasing.* Pair off with someone next to you. Devise a conversational scenario in which paraphrasing might be employed. Next, discuss and paraphrase a response for each of the following scenarios (approx. 10 mins.):
   a. "I had a dream last night. I dreamed the grandchildren came over to visit their old granddad. But that's dreams for you. Nobody comes over to see me anymore."
   b. "If you take a job, it'll just ruin our marriage. There's no way I'm going to start washing the dishes and cooking food—that's your job!"
   c. "Why should I clean up my room? It's *mine*, and I'm perfectly comfortable with it. You're just too picky."

Debriefing Questions

Write your answers to the debriefing questions in the following spaces. (approx. 10 mins.)

1. Describe your personal reaction (feelings, thoughts) to the communication exercise.

2. What did you learn about yourself in the course of this exercise?

3. What did you learn about others in the course of this exercise?

4. Name two ways in which you can use what you have learned in daily life.

The Problem-Solving Process

The problem-solving process provides opportunities to put the fourteen personal competencies, the dialogue process, and the conflict-recovery techniques into practice. The problem-solving process comprises six steps. These steps, to be effective, must be taken flexibly in accord with the particular circumstances of the problematic situation. The process, in other words, must be tailored to the specific needs of the particular group. The six steps are as follows:

1. *Define the problem.* The first step in problem solving is to recognize there is a problem. This does not mean simply admitting that a problem exists, but rather defining it in terms that are clear to all parties. Defining the problem, then, means to describe it by naming specifically the objectionable behaviors and their consequences.

2. *Identify possible solutions and generate a list.* Brainstorm a variety of solutions by raising questions like What are some possible solutions to this problem? How many ideas can we list? Remember, in brainstorming the objective is to generate as many ideas as possible in the time available and regardless of their feasibility. The more ideas the better. *All* ideas are welcome because we want to create a pool of ideas to draw on in devising a practical and effective problem-solving plan

3. *Evaluate the list of possible solutions.* This step, in which the list of possible solutions is subjected to critical examination and analysis, is actually a process of deliberation and the natural follow-up to the brainstorming process of step 2. In step 3, it is very important that all persons express their ideas and feelings about the list of proposed solutions. Each person in the group needs to be clear about which solutions are unacceptable and why. In promoting or rejecting a given solution, for example, the reasons why the solution will or will not work need to be pinpointed for discussion. In this way, positive effects or unforeseen negative effects, why a given solution does not satisfy a particular need, or why a given solution seems unfair will all become clear.

4. *Choose a proposed solution for implementation.* This step, the choice of a proposed solution, is the end product of the process of deliberation carried on in step 3, and can only really come about through *open* discussion among all the members of the group. From the openness and candor of the group, a true group choice will gradually emerge. Once a solution satisfactory to all parties has been identified and accepted, the group must give practical consideration to its implementation.

5. *Devise an implementation plan for the solution.* In this step, the group reflects on how to go about implementing the solution they have decided upon. An implementation plan is a blueprint for action: a step-by-step outline for putting the solution into effect. So, in step 5, the group discusses the series of actions called for by the solution and determines a concrete sequence of steps. The group must also specify a practical timetable for each step and designate specific tasks. Flexibility and feasibility are key dynamics in determining timetables and sequencing tasks in each step of the implementation plan. Evaluation tools are also vital for monitoring both the progress and effectiveness of the implementation plan. Both formative and summative evaluation measures are very useful, if possible. A formative evaluation measures the success of the solution as it unfolds—that is, shows the progress or lack of progress in resolving the original problem situation. A summative evaluation provides an overall assessment of the implementation plan (Fitz-Gibbon & Morris, 1987).

6. *Assess the success of the solution.* In this step, the group establishes a mutually agreeable period of time for assessing the success of the solution after its implementation. The objective in this assessment is to see how effective the solution actually was and to determine how satisfied the parties feel with it. Both the formative and summative evaluation measures discussed in connection with the implementation process come in handy here. If these measures have been taken in the course of the implementation plan, the group will now have documentation in hand about the history of the process, which will give depth and background to the formative and summative evaluations taken at this later time when the implementation plan is considered complete.

Worksheet 17

Using Dialogue in Case Analysis

(approx. total time 45 mins.)

Purpose To practice the first three skills of cultural competence (Chapters 2, 3, and 4).

Instructions Form groups of four to five people. Discuss three case examples of a diversity issue. The group can select cases from the following list, describe a new case, or use one from a previous exercise. For each case, engage in a dialogue in relation to these questions: What aspects of culture do you see in each case? (See pages 19–20.) What barriers do you see operating in each case? (See pages 43–44). What competencies would improve the interaction in each case? (See pages 61–62). Let someone in the group write down the group's answers to the questions on a separate sheet and someone else serve as spokesperson for the group in the whole-class discussion. (approx. 30 mins.)

Case examples:

• *Business office.* People from different cultures are taught to respect authority. You call a team meeting, with a desire for serious input, ideas, and feedback—even disagreement, if that's what it takes to find solutions and resolve issues. The cultural background of the team members, however, appears to hinder them in questioning or disagreeing with what they perceive as authority. How is this to be resolved?

• *County government office.* An employee from Central America refuses to follow orders from shift leads. This employee is male and the shift leads are females. He does, however, accept my orders as the unit supervisor, although I also am female. It seems that three female bosses are too much for him. Where do we go with this?

• *Factory.* In dealing with diverse cultural groups, I do not permit or condone ethnic jokes in the working environment, but one cultural group repeatedly engages in this behavior, targeting their own ethnic group. The jokes and comments are in fact degrading and demeaning. They are also counterproductive for the promotion of respect for differing cultures. The group thinks, however, that because the jokes target themselves, they are OK. What approaches are called for in resolving this issue?

• *School-district office.* A job task requires three Latino professionals to work together as a team. One is Mexican American, one Salvadoran, and the third, Puerto Rican. Each speaks Spanish as well as English. There is a great deal of animosity among the members of this group.

One member says another acts "bossy" and "aristocratic" and treats others as "servants." Another complains that one member is always "rude." The conflicts seem to relate to cultural and social-status issues. How might conflict here be addressed more effectively?

• *Hospital care facility.* Early this afternoon Mrs. Vahahrami, an East Indian in her mid-twenties, has given birth to a healthy baby boy. Following the birth of the boy, Mr. Vahahrami and his mother have come in to see the patient. In accordance with hospital procedure, the delivering doctor, Dr. Garibaldi, has had the baby dressed in hospital clothing and sent to the nursery for the night while the mother recuperates. During the labor and birthing procedures, it was necessary to draw some of Mrs. Vahahrami's blood. These procedures were met with harsh glares and a rise in tension between the patient and family and the delivering doctor.

When Dr. Garibaldi reminds Mr. and Mrs. Vahahrami that they are to abstain from sex for six weeks and recommends routine circumcision for the new infant, the patient and family all look extremely shocked and revolted, and Mrs. Vahahrami begins to weep. Throughout the day, tension between the delivering doctor and the patient and family has slowly been rising, culminating in Mrs. Vahahrami's crying episode. The family, moreover, has shown reluctance to adhere to some of the doctor's requests, and in particular Mr. Vahahrami has voiced adamant refusal to have his son circumcised.

Dr. Garibaldi is greatly confused by the agitated behavior of his patient and her family and has decided that this problem has become too great and must be dealt with. Together with those involved with him on this case, Dr. Garibaldi intends to attempt to sort out this confusion. What directions might he and his staff take?

Debriefing Questions

Write your answers to the debriefing questions in the following spaces. (approx. 15 mins.)

1. Describe your personal reaction (feelings, thoughts) to the dialogue exercise. Did a dialogue of the case examples happen in your group? Describe.

2. What did you learn about yourself in the course of this exercise?

3. What did you learn about others in the course of this exercise?

4. Name two ways in which you can use what you have learned in daily life.

In Chapter 4 we have worked with the third skill of cultural diversity competence: developing the fourteen personal competencies and the interpersonal processes of dialogue, conflict recovery, and collaborative problem solving. In Chapter 5 we practice the development of action plans for implementing cultural competence throughout the organization.

Chapter 5

Skill Four

Practicing the Design and Implementation of Organizational Strategies and Action Plans

Like skill 3, skill 4 is a "practicing skill," but unlike skill 3 and the other two, skill 4 is also an "integrating skill," in that it pulls together in a dynamic way the action of the first three skills. In this sense skill 4 is holistic and engages participants in organizationwide problem-solving activities. Skill 4 requires that participants experience, with full cognizance, working on all *three* of the levels represented by skills 1 through 3. Participants working with skill 4 techniques engage in personal, interpersonal, and organizational thinking and skill development. And they do this in the context of the practical organizational and institutional tasks they meet up with daily in their work. Skill 4, in this way, is a practice that draws together and integrates the content of all three previous skills. Skill 4 consists of developing case examples and action plans.

Developing Case Examples

In this first part of skill 4, you will practice the technique of pulling together the specific content of a real-life problem or issue in cultural diversity. Working from personal experience covering the last two years, you will write a case example documenting a cultural-diversity issue or problem.

Worksheet 18

Writing a Case Example (approx. total time 20 mins.)

Purpose To practice all four cultural-diversity competence skills in holistic action planning for implementing cultural competence throughout the organization.

Instructions Form groups of four to five people. Using the case examples from Chapter 4 as guides (pp. 73–74), let one person in the group serve as recorder to write up a new case example, on a separate sheet, and another serve as spokesperson for the group in the class discussion. (approx. 20 mins.)

Developing Action Plans

In this second part of skill 4, you will practice the technique of devising plans of action for intervening in the specific problems isolated and identified in Worksheet 18. In devising action plans, you must engage in an activity similar to that described in Chapter 4 in my discussion of step 5 of the problem-solving process. Working in small groups, you will analyze the cultural aspects and barriers for each case example. Your group will then set up a series of actions that can be programmed into a concrete sequence of steps for implementing a solution. This program must also be augmented with specific timetables and evaluation measures.

This activity of developing action plans clearly involves you in the problem-solving process of skill 3, as I have noted. Many other aspects of the understanding and practice entailed in the first three skills, however, are also called into play. In devising action plans to remedy the problems embodied in your case example, you must engage in *self-reflection* and apply your culturally sensitive *competencies* (skills), not just in the sense of addressing the case-example problem, but in the dramatic real-life sense that you will be working in a group that is itself composed of culturally diverse people. The very classroom activity becomes a dynamic focus of cultural diversity! The activity itself requires culturally diverse participants to call upon personal competencies in order to establish the effective communication necessary within the group to perform the exercise. Note, too, that in this classroom dynamic, the teams are working on an even broader skill level (a skill-4 level) in that, in order to complete the exercise with success, you must develop an organizational plan with objectives and measures of evaluation for the three skill levels on which barriers exist. In this respect, you will engage in the process of planning policies that will effect real organizational change—and you must do this in a setting that is itself culturally diverse. This is clearly *holistic* activity for holistic organizational change, and it begins right in the classroom or training workshop itself.

Worksheet 19

Devising Action Plans (approx. total time 60 mins.)

Purpose To practice action-plan development for implementing cultural competence throughout the organization.

Instructions In your small group, summarize the main points of the case example developed in Worksheet 18. Then outline the aspects of culture that relate to the conflict. Are any of the six barriers evident? Using the following outline, develop an action plan for the case example. Record the action plan in the blank outline that follows the example. (approx. 30 mins.)

Action Plan Outline

1. Personal and interpersonal level
   a. Objectives and goals: Identify an objective or goal that would improve the interaction in the case example. Identify the competencies that would improve the interaction in the case example.
   b. Action steps: Identify specific activities that will promote the achievement of the objective. See the organizational strategies suggested in the section following this worksheet.
   c. Timetable: Set up a schedule for achieving the objective.
   d. Measures of progress: Identify specific measures that demonstrate the achievement of the objective.

2. Organizationwide level
   a. Objectives and goals: Discuss and identify an organizationwide objective or goal.
   b. Action steps: Specify activities that promote the achievement of the objective. See the organizational strategies suggested in the section following this worksheet.
   c. Timetable: Set up a schedule for carrying out the action.
   d. Measures of progress: Identify specific measures that demonstrate the achievement of the objective.

Example:

Summary: A school with a large Hispanic population is planning to celebrate Cinco de Mayo with strolling mariachi musicians. The classroom teachers spend time preparing the children for the classroom visits of the mariachis. During the event, however, the musicians skip some of the classrooms that have fewer Hispanic children. The children in these classrooms feel left out and disappointed.

Cultural issues and barriers: In this case example we can identify two aspects of culture: art and expressive forms and social-group interaction patterns. Among the barriers, stereotyping, verbal barriers, judgment, stress, and organizational barriers are to be noted. The children in the classrooms that are not visited by the mariachis feel disappointed, neglected, and devalued by the school. The circumstance that the school fails to include all of the children of all of the classes gives rise to the central problem—lack of inclusion.

1. Personal and interpersonal level
   a. Objectives and goals: The following personal competencies are relevant in this case example: To show empathy. To listen carefully. To manage personal biases and stereotypes. To be nonjudgmental. To assume complexity. To be flexible. To show respect. To be resourceful.
   b. Action steps: Provide cultural competence training for everyone in the school.
   c. Timetable: Call an in-service before the semester begins in fall.
   d. Measures of progress: Surveys indicate all students feel included in school activities and feel valued by the school staff. Staff feel positive about working at the school and feel part of an important team. These measures of progress should be documented.

2. Organizationwide level
   a. Objectives and goals: To design school programs that are wholly inclusionary.
   b. Action steps:
      • Recruit diverse employees.
      • Create a central school area featuring a calendar and perhaps a globe that show how all groups are represented and how all groups figure in the larger picture.
      • Hold school cultural-awareness assemblies for everyone's participation—active participation insofar as possible.
      • Encourage kids to write essays about cultural awareness problems, incidents, and issues.
      • Sponsor culturally sensitive films with follow-up discussions that pinpoint relevant diversity issues.
      • Promote cultural awareness projects, especially those that put someone in the other person's shoes and demonstrate what it's like to be somebody else.
   c. Timetable: Schedule cultural events at three-month intervals throughout the school year.
   d. Measures of progress:

- Surveys to show parent involvement.
- Student responses on essays documenting how included they may or may not feel.
- Teacher evaluations documenting their views of the program and its success.
- Documentation of the increase or decrease of student behavioral problems as an indicator of progress.

Your Case Example and Action Plan

Case example summary:

Cultural issues and barriers:

1. Personal and interpersonal level
   a. Objectives and goals:

   b. Action steps:

   c. Timetable:

   d. Measures of progress:

2. Organizationwide level
   a. Objectives and goals:

   b. Action steps:

   c. Timetable:

d. Measures of progress:

Debriefing Questions

Write your answers to the debriefing questions in the following spaces.
(approx. 30 mins.)

1. Let the spokesperson for each group present in turn their case analysis and action plan to the whole class.

2. List any personal competencies that you found at your command in carrying out this exercise.

3. Describe your personal reaction (feelings, thoughts) to the exercise. Did a dialogue in connection with the case examples occur in your group? If so, describe.

4. What did you learn about others in the course of this exercise?

5. Name two ways in which you can use what you have learned in daily life.

Organizational Strategies

Internal Organizational Strategies

The following strategies (adapted from Fernandez, 1991; Kanter, 1977; Morrison, 1992; Loder & Rosener, 1991; Abramms-Mezoff & Johns, 1989; Copeland, 1988) promote the development of diversity competence inside the organization and focus on the relations among employees, managers, supervisors—ideally, *all* the personnel of the organization. Framed as a list of five general guidelines, the strategies offer possible approaches or directions an organization might take in addressing internal issues and problems in cultural diversity.

1. Maintain cultural awareness and support at all levels of the organization.

   - Provide cultural diversity training for all employees, including CEOs, supervisors, and all managers.

   - Provide ongoing follow-up forums on cultural issues and problem solving.

   - Provide mentoring and coaching in the identification of cultural issues and in the solving of cultural problems.

   - Provide support in the formation of self-help groups and in networking among employees.

   - Provide encouragement for culture-sensitive social events and the celebration of ethnic holidays.

   - Establish a strategic diversity-planning and implementation committee composed of representatives from *all* divisions, departments, and levels of the organization.

   - Establish culturally diverse management teams.

   - Incorporate a diversity-training component into the orientation sessions for all new employees.

   - Hire a diversity-training consultant to present at least six hours of cultural-diversity training to all managers *each year*.

   - Create an office or appoint a staff manager responsible for cultural diversity issues.

   - Set annual cultural diversity goals in hiring and promotion for each of the company's divisions—in both staffing and line jobs.

   - Review policies to ascertain whether they appreciate and support cultural diversity.

   - Monitor working procedures with employees who resist changes in discriminatory employment practices, that is to say, keep close watch over employees whose behavior has proven discriminatory in the past.

2. Recruit culturally diverse employees.

- Establish ongoing outreach programs in the community to recruit culturally diverse employees and to establish your organization's reputation as a leader in cultural diversity.

- Establish a culturally diverse recruitment team whose members represent the cultural diversity of the community.

- If you have a college recruitment program, 10 percent of the colleges and universities represented should be schools with at least a 50 percent minority enrollment.

- Develop a "critical mass" or "dynamic mix" of ethnic or otherwise culturally diverse staff and clients in order to ensure the cultural diversity of programs in your organization.

3. Provide career development opportunities for *all* employees.

- Establish a mentoring, coaching, or "buddy" system for all new employees to learn the organization's goals, values, policies, and procedures.

- Provide coaching and tutoring mechanisms to enhance individual and work-team effectiveness.

- Provide education incentives and ESL training. Fund this with tuition vouchers, if possible—it's good for the organization in every way.

- Provide candid and accurate feedback to employees about job performance, especially in matters of cultural diversity.

- Establish performance evaluations based on actual documented achievement and results (not on personality, work style, or supervisor's personal rapport with the employee).

- Establish a system that rewards behavior that supports and makes use of cultural diversity (the formation of multicultural work teams would be an example of such use).

- Establish information mechanisms for finding out why employees leave the organization (exit interviews, for example).

- Encourage employees to work with new technology or to create new products, services, or processes.

- Make development planning a part of the annual goal-setting process rather than a part of performance appraisal—the latter centered on individual whim and fancy will prove haphazard and random at best, while development planning as a part of organizational procedure will be more systemic and reliable.

- Establish an expenditure budget for personal self-development for every employee, one that can be accessed ad hoc without a lengthy approval process.

4. Create flexible benefit and service plans that meet the needs of culturally diverse employees.

- Establish optional insurance plans.
- Provide information about day-care and elder-care options.
- Provide variable retirement plans (early, partial, or phased).
- Encourage employee ownership through gain sharing, stock options, and other incentive programs.
- Provide family-friendly benefit policies, employee assistance programs, and long-term mutual commitments.
- Provide alternative work-time options such as flextime, compressed work weeks, flexplace, and telecommunication, as well as job sharing to accommodate employee needs.

5. Monitor the change process.

- Establish a system to monitor culturally diverse recruitment, career development, and promotion in the organization.
- Establish a system in the organization to monitor cultural diversity trends and issues in the local community.

External Organizational Strategies

The following strategies (adapted from Krebs & Kunimoto, 1994; Lum, 1996) promote the development of diversity competence in an organization's external relationships. They focus accordingly on the relations of the organization with other organizations, with culturally diverse individuals in the community, as well as with culturally diverse clients and customers. Framed as a list of four general guidelines, the strategies that follow offer possible approaches or directions an organization might take in addressing external issues and problems in cultural diversity. Generally speaking, the changes in the organization called for by these issues and problems will involve, among other things, the establishment of wider linguistic resources for the staff, as well as the improvement of their cultural awareness, understanding, and skills. Beyond these measures, the organization will need to modify current policies and services in order to achieve a better overall "cultural fit" with clients and customers of greater cultural diversity. The four general guidelines reflect these concerns.

1. Establish effective relationships with client communities.

- Establish a steering committee made up of organization staff, culturally diverse community leaders, practitioners, and educators to facilitate program development.

- Establish support bases with the agency administrator, governing board, and ethnic-community organizations in order to ensure that service is provided in a culturally appropriate way.

- Promote community organizations, such as mutual-assistance associations, to serve as vehicles for managing culturally diverse training programs in social skills. Such programs in their educational thrust regularly prove very effective in preventing troublesome issues and problems in cultural diversity.

- Call on the help of indigenous community workers and natural community caretakers such as ministers, employee relatives, prominent community members, and family physicians. This practice dignifies the community and enriches the organization.

- Study typical family structures and hierarchies to become acquainted with appropriate client kin-relationships in order to provide useful information and support resources for the organization.

- Establish links with at least two ethnic organizations in the community for job referrals as well as for posting your job notices to reach their culturally diverse clients and customers.

- Foster friendly neighborhood sharing and support services linking clients to schools, churches, and other organizations in a culturally diverse way.

- Foster bilingual and bicultural programs as essential services in mixed ethnic or otherwise culturally diverse communities.

- Solicit community input and participation in organizational policy making. This initiative implies comprehensive orientation programs for organization board members, as well as open access and communication between organization administration and decision makers and community representatives.

- Foster relationships that link the organization with other culturally diverse organizations for mutual information.

- Foster the development of ethnic networks within community centers to promote interaction in a bilingual and culturally diverse way that is appropriate to the community.

- Promote the official and highly visible presence of the organization at local restaurants, businesses, community events, and other venues of popular social interaction in order to establish rapport and warm community relations.

- Locate public and private organizations that function as service agencies providing health care, day care, employment services, and the like, near the culturally diverse communities they serve.

2. Review the ethics and social responsibility of the organization.

   - Promote corporate social-responsibility efforts that are aimed at the overall long-term improvement of the social environment the organization provides.

   - Establish criteria for measuring the organization's impact on the physical environment.

   - Set up ethics committees for careful deliberation when complex moral issues or dilemmas arise. These committees should typically examine available options as well as their implications for all parties concerned, always taking relevant issues of cultural diversity into account.

   - Provide mechanisms to ensure that ethics committees in their interaction demonstrate respect for culturally diverse perspectives by providing a safe environment for group members to share their varying cultural experience in the common evaluation of ethical issues. Effective relations among the culturally diverse members of ethics committees themselves are essential if these groups are to engage in effective deliberation of bioethical issues that affect the community at large.

   - Make it procedural for ethics committees to seek relevant information from sources external to the committee and to take into regular account the relevant cultural perspective of all individuals involved in the issues under examination.

3. Strive for customer and client satisfaction in a culturally diverse way.

   - Establish organizational programs in which personnel can truly partner with their internal and external clients and customers.

   - Initiate policies that encourage personnel to be sensitive and alert to their clients' and customers' future needs in order to better serve them. Culturally diverse sensitivities are obviously very useful here.

- Establish as policy regular debriefing sessions for personnel in order to document information about their internal and external clients and customers.

- Establish criteria for gauging client and customer satisfaction.

4. Work respectfully and responsively with a culturally diverse clientele.

- Encourage clients to participate actively in making decisions about their care.

- Provide culturally sensitive support groups to help clients cope with severe life stress through communication. These support groups would ideally be culturally diverse and provide relevant information about health-care methods and services, problem-solving interaction, referral services, friendly visits, and assistance in making choices about the various kinds of care available.

- Devise culturally diverse communication strategies vis-à-vis the external community in order to establish good public relations with the relevant culturally diverse population. Ideal culturally diverse strategies would provide readily intelligible information to the community in various ways such as annual reports, health education publications, press releases, or local advertisements. These strategies would also function as a conduit for information about issues in the external community pertinent to the organization, and they would promote coordination between the organization and key members of the external community.

- Make it procedural that all health promotion efforts arise out of a clear understanding of and sensitivity to the diverse cultural influences on the health beliefs and practices of the target audiences.

- Make it a matter of organizational awareness—on the level of reflex and spontaneous conditioning—that cultural roots run very deep and will be operative in audience interpretation and response no matter how clearly "rational" and "sensible" the goals and objectives of a particular program or campaign may be.

- Select target audiences with great care for culturally homogeneity when planning programs and campaigns in order to ensure maximum relevance and effect for campaign and program messages.

- Design strategies that are culturally sensitive and promote the long-term involvement of the target audience and the institutionalization of key activities within the target community when planning programs and campaigns.

- Establish a clear set of program or campaign activities and a diversity of media (products) to promote program or campaign objectives. Price, placement, and promotion are vital factors in the selection of these activities and media. They must be *affordable* in terms of financial and psychological cost; they must be *attractive* to the audience, designed to grab and hold audience attention; and they must be *informative,* telling the audience how, when, and where the program's or campaign's materials are accessible.

- Set up process-evaluation procedures for monitoring and assessing program or campaign activities in order to isolate and identify efforts that require refinement.

- Chart a step-by-step service-delivery system for culturally diverse clients. This system may call for an increase in qualified bilingual and bicultural staff, the location of more accessible facilities, community outreach programs, and so on.

- Schedule an increase of culturally appropriate services for client populations.

- Make organizational provision for Southeast Asian clients who may establish a vicarious family relationship with organization personnel. This cultural process can involve assigning the worker a position of kinship within the family.

- Consider initiatives like the following four, which proved effective among Latinos (can be adapted for all culture groups in a community): (1) Spanish-language radio and television programming—a major vehicle of communication in the Chicano/Mexicano community; (2) a bilingual manual of preventive health care—prepared first in Spanish and then translated into English to retain a distinctly Chicano/Mexicano perspective; (3) educational coffee klatches and teas, called *meriendas educativas,* organized from within the community to promote group mental health among low-income Spanish-speaking women; and (4) learning fairs (*fiestas educativas*)—all-day health workshops for high-risk Hispanics.

- Link with local churches, community youth centers, and schools to establish peer support groups for Mexican-American youth who have little or no family support. These links can provide functions and support analogous to the family but with a special focus on bilingual competence and education, important factors in a Mexican-American cultural setting.

- Increase communication and promote mental health through educational initiatives, media programming, small informal gatherings, and health fairs.

- Set up accessible community sites that offer concrete practical help.

- Destigmatize services by changing their names—for example, changing "mental health services" to "family outreach services."

- Provide a friendly bilingual staff, offer refreshments, and select office decor that reflects an appropriate ethnic or culturally diverse setting.

- Create organizational procedures for supplying appropriate mediators from the culturally diverse community in cases in which clients are uncomfortable or unwilling to accept organization personnel as mediators.

Appendix

Aspects of the Mainstream
U.S. Culture*

1. History: Mainstream culture in the United States derives from the Anglo-Saxon culture of the English who colonized America.

2. Social group interaction patterns:
   - Intragroup: English immigrants institutionalized English culture in the United States.
   - Intergroup: Starting in colonial times, White members of U.S. national culture displayed "nativism" toward groups perceived as different: foreigners, Jews, Catholics, Blacks.

3. Social status factors: Middle-class culture is the norm, yet there are a range of classes from poor through working to middle and upper. Since the 1970s the upper and poor classes have been growing, with the middle class declining.

4. Value orientations:
   - Emphasis on patriarchal nuclear family.
   - Emphasis on doing, "getting things done" (keeping busy).
   - Emphasis on measurable and visible accomplishments.
   - Emphasis on individual choice, responsibility and achievement.
   - Emphasis on self-reliance and self-motivation.
   - Emphasis on pragmatism: "If an idea works, use it."
   - Emphasis on the new (and change).
   - Emphasis on causal agent; things do not just happen.
   - Emphasis on equality, informality and fair play simultaneously with widespread nativism and micro and macro institutional discrimination.

*by Mikel Hogan-Garcia, 1991. Adapted from Bellah et al., 1985; Hodge et al., 1975; Rose, 1989; and Stewart & Bennet, 1991.

- Emphasis on competition.
- Emphasis on direct communication.
- Emphasis on controlling nature; nature should serve humans.
- Emphasis on materialism, machines and technology, and progress.
- Emphasis on private property (valued more than human rights).
- Emphasis on precise reckoning of time, which is perceived as linear.

5. Language and communication:
   - Verbal: English language spoken; most do not speak second language, nor is it valued. Low context communication style: direct, explicit, and informal.
   - Nonverbal: Not recognized as being as important as verbal communication.

6. Family life processes: Traditionally, patriarchal nuclear family structure. Currently much variation in family structure due to social and cultural change.
   - Gender roles: Traditionally male job holder, female homemaker, but changing gender roles since 1960s.
   - Occupations: Varies with socioeconomic status.
   - Education: Varies with socioeconomic status.
   - Marriage customs: Changing; marriage in later twenties increasing.
   - Divorce practice: High rate of divorce and serial marriage common.
   - Parenting beliefs and practices: Emphasis on individualism and self-reliance.

7. Healing beliefs and practices: Body seen as biological organism.
8. Religion: Protestant religions, biblical tradition emphasized.
9. Art and expressive forms: Music and visual art emphasized, not verbal arts, for example.
10. Diet: Hamburgers, hot dogs, but diets vary regionally.
11. Recreation: Sports, TV, and many other options (much variation).
12. Clothes: Styles change with time and place (region).

References

Abremms-Mezoff, B., & Johns, D. (1989, May). Success strategies. *Supervision,* 1–15.

Bellah, R., Madsen, R., Sullivan, W., Swidler, A., & Tipton, S. (Eds.). (1985). *Habits of the heart.* New York: Harper & Row.

Bodley, J. H. (1996). *Anthropology and contemporary human problems* (3rd ed.) Mountain View, CA: Mayfield.

Brislen, R. (1986). *Intercultural interactions: A practical guide.* Beverly Hills, CA: Sage.

Brookfield, S. (1990). *The skillful teacher.* San Francisco, CA: Jossey-Bass.

Copeland, L. (1988, June). Valuing diversity, Part 1. *Personnel,* 52–60.

Copeland, L. (1988, July). Valuing diversity, Part 2. *Personnel,* 44–49.

DeAnda, D. (1984). Bicultural socialization: Factors affecting the minority experience. *National Association of Social Workers,* 101–107.

Delgado, R., & Stefancic, J. (1997). *Critical White studies: Looking behind the mirror.* Philadelphia, PA: Temple University Press.

Eddy, E., & Partridge, W. (1987). *Applied anthropology in America.* New York: Columbia University Press.

Essed, P. (1991). *Understanding everyday racism: An interdisciplinary theory.* Beverly Hills, CA: Sage.

Feagin, J. (1991). The continuing significance of race: Antiblack discrimination in public places. *American Sociological Review, 56,* 101–116.

Feagin, J. (1996). Racial and ethnic relations (5th ed.). Englewood Cliffs, NJ: Prentice-Hall.

Fernandez, J. P. (1991). *Managing a diverse work force.* Lexington, MA: Lexington Books.

Ferraro, G. (1990). *The cultural dimension of international business.* Englewood Cliffs, NJ: Prentice-Hall.

Fine, M. (1990). "The public" in public schools: The social construction/constriction of moral communities. *Journal of Social Issues, 46*(1), 107–119.

Fitz-Gibbon, C., & Morris, L. (1987). *How to design a program evaluation.* Newbury Park, CA: Sage.

Foster, B., et al. (1988, April). Workforce diversity and business. *Training and Development Journal,* 38–42.

Gochenour, T. (1993). *Beyond experience: The experiential approach to cross-cultural education.* Yarmouth, ME: Intercultural Press.

Goldstein, J., & Leopold, M. (1990). Corporate culture versus ethnic culture. *Personnel Journal,* 88–92.

Hall, E., & Hall, M. (1987). *Hidden differences: Doing business with the Japanese.* New York: Doubleday.

Hamada, T., & Sibley, W. E. (Eds.). (1994). *Anthropological perspectives on organizational culture.* New York: University Press of America.

Helms, J. (1989). Considering some methodological issues in racial identity counseling research. *The Counseling Psychologist, 17,* 227–252.

Hill-Burnett, J. (1987). Anthropological knowledge through application. In E. Eddy & W. Partridge, Eds., *Applied anthropology in America.* New York: Columbia University Press.

Hodge, J., et al. (1975). The cultural basis of racism. Berkeley, CA: Two Riders Press.

Hofstede, G. (1990). *Cultures and organizations.* New York: McGraw-Hill.

Hogan-Garcia, M. (1991). Teaching theory and practice: a constructivist approach. *Practicing Anthropologist, 14,* 23–33.

Hogan-Garcia, M. (1994, August). A method for introducing the skill of diversity competence in an introduction to human services course. *Journal of Counseling and Human Services Professions,* 25–43.

Hogan-Garcia, M. (1995). An anthropological approach to multicultural diversity training. *The Journal of Applied Behavioral Science, 31*(4), 490–505.

Hogan-Garcia, M., & Wright, J. (1989). Communication and multicultural awareness: An interactional training model. *Journal of Counseling and Human Service Professions, 3*(2), 29–39.

Hogan-Garcia, M., Wright, J., & Corey, G. (1991, September/October). A multicultural perspective in an undergraduate human services program. *Journal of Counseling and Development, 70,* 86–90.

Hudson Institute (1987). *Workforce 2000.* Indianapolis, Indiana.

Ivey, A., & Gluckstern, N. (1982). *Basic attending skills.* North Amherst, MA: Microtraining Associates.

Jamieson, D., & O'Mara, J. (1991). *Managing workforce 2000.* San Francisco: Jossey-Bass.

Jordan, A. (1994). Practicing anthropology in corporate America: Consulting on organization culture. *NAPA Bulletin, 14.*

Kanter, R. M. (1977). *Men and women of the corporation.* New York: Basic Books.

Kanter, R. M. (1983). *The change masters.* New York: Simon & Schuster.

Kanter, R. M. (1989). *When giants learn to dance.* New York: Simon & Schuster.

Killman, R. (1987). *Beyond the quick fix.* San Francisco: Jossey-Bass.

Kogod, S. (1994). In Jordan, A. *Practicing anthropology in corporate America; consulting on organization culture.* NAPA Bulletin, 14.

Kohls, L. R. (1984). *Survival kit for overseas living.* Yarmouth, ME: Intercultural Press, Inc.

Krebs, G., & Kunimoto, E. (1994). *Effective communication in multicultural health care settings.* Newbury Park, CA: Sage.

Lamphere, L. (Ed.). (1992). *Structuring diversity: Ethnographic perspectives on the new immigration.* Chicago: The University of Chicago Press.

Leiberman, L. (1997). *"Race" 1997 and 2001: A race odyssey.* Arlington, VA: American Anthropological Association, GAD Module Series in Teaching Anthropology, Module 3.

Leiberman, L., & Rice, P. C. (1997). *Race or clines?* Arlington, VA: American Anthropological Association, GAD Module Series in Teaching Anthropology, Module 2.

Leininger, M. (1995). Transcultural nursing: Concepts, theories, research, and practice. Columbus, OH: McGraw-Hill and Greyden Press.

Lett, J. (1987). *The human enterprise: A critical introduction to anthropological theory.* Boulder, CO: Westview Press.

Levinson, B., Foley, D., & Holland, D. (1996). *The cultural production of the educated person.* New York: State University of New York Press.

Loden, M., & Rosener, J. (1991). *Workforce America! Managing employee diversity as a vital resource.* Homewood, IL: Business One Irwin.

Lum, D. (1996). *Social work practice and people of color.* Pacific Grove, CA: Brooks/Cole.

Malott, R., Tillema, M., & Glenn, S. (1978). *Behavior analysis and behavior modification: An introduction.* Kalamazoo, MI: Behaviordelia.

McIntosh, P. (1993). Examining unearned privilege. *On Campus with Women, 22,* 9–10.

Mehr, J. (1992). *Human services concepts and intervention strategies.* Boston: Allyn & Bacon.

Montagu, A. (1974). *The concept of race,* 2nd ed. New York, NY: The Free Press.

Morgan, G., & Ramirez, R. (1983). Action learning: a holographic metaphor for guiding social change. *Human Relations, 37,* 1–28.

Morrison, A. (1992). *The new leaders: Guidelines on leadership diversity in America.* San Francisco: Jossey-Bass.

Nader, L. (Ed.). (1994). *Essays on controlling processes.* Berkeley, CA: Kroeber Anthropological Society Papers (77).

Nelton, S. (1988, July). Meet your new workforce. *Nation's Business,* 14–21.

Padilla, A. (1986). Acculturation and stress among immigrants and later generation individuals. *The Quality of Urban Life*. New York: Gruyter.

Paige, R. M. (1993). *Education for the intercultural experience*. Yarmouth, ME: Intercultural Press.

Partridge, W. (1987). Toward a theory of practice. In E. Eddy & W. Partridge, Eds., *Applied anthropology in America*. New York: Columbia University Press.

Pederson, P. (1988). *A handbook for developing multicultural awareness*. Alexandria, VA: American Association for Counseling and Development.

Phinney, J. (1989, May). Stages of ethnic identity development in minority group adolescents. *Journal of Early Adolescence, 9*(1-2), 34–49.

Phinney, J. (1990). Ethnic identity in adolescents and adults: Review of research. *Psychological Bulletin, 108*(3), 499–514.

Phinney, J., & Rotherman, M. (Eds.). (1987). *Children's ethnic socialization*. Newbury Park, CA: Sage.

Root, M. (Ed.). (1992). Racially mixed people in America. Newbury Park: Sage.

Rose, D. (1989). *Patterns of American culture*. Philadelphia: University of Pennsylvania Press.

Rose, D. (1990). *Living the ethnographic life*. Newbury Park, CA: Sage.

Rosen, R. (1991). *The healthy company: Eight strategies to develop people, productivity, and products*. New York: Putnam.

Rosener, J. (1998). *America's competitive secret: Women managers*. New York: Oxford University Press.

Schon, D. (1987). *Educating the reflective practitioner*. San Francisco: Jossey-Bass.

Schwartzman, H. B. (1993). *Ethnography in organizations*. Newbury Park, CA: Sage.

Sikkema, M., & Niyekawa, A. (1987). *Design for cross-cultural learning*. Yarmouth, ME: Intercultural Press.

Sleeter, C., & McLaren, P. (1995). *Multicultural education, critical pedagogy, and the politics of difference*. New York: State University of New York Press.

Smith, T. (1993). *Parcival's briefcase: Six practices and a new philosophy for healthy organizational change*. San Francisco: Chronicle Books.

Spector, R. (1996). *Cultural diversity in health and illness*. Stamford, CT: Appleton & Lange.

Stewart, E., & Bennet, M. (1991). *American cultural patterns*. Yarmouth, ME: Intercultural Press.

Sue, D. (1981). *Counseling the culturally different*. New York: Wiley.

Tatum, B. D. (1992). Talking about race, learning about racism: The application of racial identity development theory in the classroom. *Harvard Educational Review, 62*(1), 1–24.

Tatum, B. D. (1997). *Why Are All the Black Kids Sitting Together in the Cafeteria?* New York: Basic Books

Thomas, R. R. (1996). *Redefining diversity*. New York: American Management Association.

Walck, C. L., & Jordan, A. T. (Eds.). (1995). Managing diversity: Anthropology's contribution to theory and practice [special issue]. *Journal of Applied Behavioral Science, 31,* 1–247.

Wali, A., & Khan, N. (1997). Inserting "culture" into multiculturalism: Conversations at the Field Museum, Chicago. *Anthropology Today, 13*(4), 9–12.

Wright, S. (1994). *Anthropology of organizations*. New York: Routledge.

Wulff, R., & Fiske, S. (1987). *Anthropological praxis: Translating knowledge into action*. Boulder, CO: Westview Press.

Index

TO THE OWNER OF THIS BOOK:

We hope that you have found *The Four Skills of Cultural Diversity Competence* useful. So that this book can be improved in a future edition, would you take the time to complete this sheet and return it? Thank you.

School and address: _____

Department: _____

Instructor's name: _____

1. What I like most about this book is: _____

_____

_____

2. What I like least about this book is: _____

_____

_____

3. My general reaction to this book is: _____

_____

4. The name of the course in which I used this book is: _____

_____

5. Were all of the chapters of the book assigned for you to read? _____

   If not, which ones weren't? _____

6. In the space below, or on a separate sheet of paper, please write specific suggestions for improving this book and anything else you'd care to share about your experience in using the book.

_____

_____

_____

_____

_____

_____

Optional:

Your name: _____ Date: _____

May Wadsworth Publishing Company quote you, either in promotion for *The Four Skills of Cultural Diversity Competence* or in future publishing ventures?

Yes: _____ No: _____

Sincerely,

Mikel Hogan-Garcia

FOLD HERE

- -

BUSINESS REPLY MAIL
FIRST CLASS   PERMIT NO. 358   PACIFIC GROVE, CA

POSTAGE WILL BE PAID BY ADDRESSEE

ATT: *Mikel Hogan-Garcia* _____

Wadsworth Publishing Company
10 Davis Drive
Belmont, California 94002

- -

FOLD HERE